The Logic of Murderous Rampages

*& Other Essays on Violence
& its Prevention*

ALSO BY JANE GILGUN

Children's Books

Busjacked!
Emma and her Forever Person
Five Little Cygnets Cross the Bundoran Road
Patrick and the Magic Mountain
The King's Toast
The Little Pig Who Didn't go to Market
The Picking Flower Garden
Thorns Have Roses: A Story of Recovery from Clergy Abuse
Turtle Night at Playa Grande
Will the Soccer Star

Books

Child Sexual Abuse: From Harsh Realities to Hope
Children with Serious Conduct Issues
Hannah Robinson: The Celebrated Beauty of Her Day
I Want to Show You: Poems
On Being a Sh*t: Unkind Deeds & Cover-Ups in Everyday Life
The NEATS: A Child & Family Assessment

Manuals

Lemons or Lemonades? An Anger Workbook for Kids
Leomons or Lemonade? An Anger Workbook for Teens
Readiness to Adopt Children with Special Needs
The CASPARS: Clinical Assessment Tools for Client Risks & Strengths

Jane Gilgun is a professor and writer. She has many books, articles, and assessment tools available through on-line bookstores and social media websites.

The Logic of Murderous Rampages

& Other Essays on Violence & its Prevention

JANE F. GILGUN, PHD, LICSW

Createspace

Copyright © 2012 by Jane F. Gilgun
jgilgun@gmail.com

The rights of Jane Gilgun to be identified as the author of this work have been asserted by her in accordance with the Copyright Designs and Patents Act of 1988.

All rights reserved. No part of this publication may be reproduced, stored in retrieval systems, or transmitted in any form or by any means, electronic, mechanical, photocopying, recording, or otherwise, without the prior written permission of the copyright owner, except for brief quotes in reviews, articles, and blogs.

Gilgun, Jane F.
The Logic of Murderous Rampages
& Other Essays on Violence & Its Prevention

The essays in this book have appeared in e-bookstores such as Kindle, Barnes & Noble, Apple iPad, Scribd.com, and Smashwords.

Cover Photo by Jane Gilgun: The site of the execution of Daniel O'Connell, leader of the 1916 Irish Rising, Kilmainham Jail, Dublin, Ireland.

1. Interpersonal Violence 2. Violence Prevention
3. Mass Murderers 4. Rape 5. Development
of Violent Behaviors
6. Childhood aggression 7. Resilience

ISBN-13: 978-1480009332
ISBN-10: 1480009334

Createspace

Visit Amazon Kindle, Google Books, iBooks,
& other Internet booksellers
to discover other books, articles, and children's stories
by Jane Gilgun that you may enjoy.

Foreword

This book is a collection of essays that I have written over several years. The essays show what I have learned about the meanings of violence to perpetrators, the development of violent behaviors, and the prevention of violence. For more than 30 years, I have interviewed perpetrators and survivors of interpersonal violence. My purpose was to understand violence from their points of view.

Acts of violence that mystify outsiders not only make sense but often are compelling to those who commit violence. Lawson, for example, found in her review of qualitative research on sex offenders' views on child sexual abuse that sex with children brought intense emotional gratification, sexual pleasure, and a sense of intimacy and even love. Some offenders reported a powerful and almost overwhelming desire to be sexual with children.

Research has identified a sense of entitlement as elements in many forms of violence, such as physical aggression against women, child sexual abuse, rape, murder, and attempted murder. In my own research, I found that some sex offenders view themselves as entitled to having sex with others without including others in their decisions. A man, "What's the big deal about rape? I raped my wife all the time" (Gilgun, 1998).

Another man said, "If I can't get them this way [through mutual consent] then the other way to get them is, you know, to just grab them." Drawing from ideas about "loose" women for whom rape supposedly has no meaning, his account of his rapes is permeated with an ideology of supremacy and beliefs about women as sexual objects for men.

A desire to control family members to the point of physical aggression and murder is a common experience for perpetrators. Violence as a means of gaining respect of violent peers and the fearful respect of those whom they terrorize are other meanings that violence has to perpetrators. Katz identified a sense of righteousness, thrills, enjoyment and satisfaction of getting away with a violent act that was difficult to pull off, being a badass man, and maintaining power and control over others as the meanings that the men he interviewed attributed to the violence they committed.

The violence women commit is far less researched then men's. Women appear to commit far less physical violence than men. For example, compared to men, they rarely appear in news stories and statistics about violent acts. In addition, there are beliefs about female non-aggression that may actually foster less violent behaviors as compared to men. On the other hand, women do commit violent acts, but often their violence appears to be a function of the socialization as women. A 32 year-old woman I interviewed, for example, was a youth minister who had a sexual relationship with a teenage girl who was part of her youth group. The woman said the girl wanted to have sex with her and to turn her away would have hurt the girl. The woman elaborated,

> I didn't want to abandon her. I will take shit to kingdom come before I will bail out.... In some ways that is very, very strong to my religious point of view. It's very strong that you be there for people. It is very strong that that's the spiritual connection and understanding of who Jesus Christ was. He didn't bail out. He didn't go when he, and he didn't maybe have his self protection up either, when it really comes down to the story. And so religiously and morally, it, it, yeah, that's where I'm at.

Other researchers, too, have noted that meanings that women attribute to their violence are related to a sense of caring, as distorted as this caring may be. Women's identity as women is far less tied to aggression and being in charge. Sometimes women's violence is in reaction to male physical aggression. Women and men may be similar in terms of how they use words and exclusionary actions to control and dominate others, however.

In summary, violence has many possible meanings to perpetrators and to those who are survivors of violence. Many of these meanings could be connected to gender role socialization and internalized beliefs that are widely held in U.S. culture. Whatever the analysis proposed in this present research might produce in terms of a model of the meanings of violence to perpetrators, the results will make important contributions to effective policies, programs, and interventions. The understanding the meanings of violence to perpetrators is fundamental to prevention and intervention.

Persons act out in violent ways because they have belief system that tells them acts of violence are what people do to accomplish their goals and they have no competing belief systems that guide them to think long and short-term about consequences for themselves and for the persons who are the targets of violence. Their developmental histories have nothing to do with their acting in violent ways. I have interviewed many survivors of violence who do not act out violently. They like anyone else may think violent thoughts but short and long-term consequences immediately come into awareness. They choose not to be violent.

In my research, I have found that the common developmental factor in persons who commit violent acts is a belief in violence and a lack of beliefs that lead them to rein in actions that follow from their pro-violence beliefs. Many people come from abusive families. Most of them do not become abusive.

Many people who commit violent acts, however, have minimal abuse in their backgrounds. Some have fewer risks for violence than I do. They, however, have pro-violent beliefs, a lack of beliefs that counter the pro-violence beliefs, and a life-long history of not sharing personal, sensitive information, an incapacity to reflect upon the events in their lives, and a lack of imagination in terms of thinking about what their actions might mean to others. They also do not identify with pro-social others and in fact may admire others who get away with putting one over on others, beating others out of a buck, and in general going their own way without regard for others. It can take a lot to get them to face the harm they cause and they may believe until they die that what they did is just how things are.

In addition to pro-violence beliefs, the difference between people with abuse in their backgrounds who become violent and those who don't is the capacity to confide personal, sensitive information to other people and find it helps. These confidant relationships are long term and provide persons who have experienced abuse with role models, value systems, and often personal and vocational skills. They usually reflect upon their own actions and have the imaginations to understand what their actions might mean to others. They are willing to change their behaviors when they realize their behaviors are harmful.

Gender comes into play in these factors, which researchers label "protective factors." Boys and men, more so than women and girls, learn through wide-spread belief systems that they are supposed to be strong and not show weakness. Many boys and men have learned to feel ashamed of such emotional states as sadness, hurt, loneliness, and worthlessness. They are afraid to talk about these emotions for fears of being labeled weak sissies. They make take on a mask of toughness and impermeability which can limit their capacities to empathize with others, to develop the imaginations to think through consequences for themselves and others, and to care about others and themselves. Such persons are on the brink of acting out pro-violence beliefs that all of us have because they have not developed the foundations of belief systems that counter pro-violence beliefs.

I also have found how important accountability is, and accountability is part of the present book. We all do things that hurt ourselves and others. This is part of being human. Accountability, admitting what we have done is wrong, apologies, and changing are ways are key to living in harmony with ourselves and others. Accountability leads to re-building relationships after a breakdown that harmful behaviors cause. Accountability rests on values, such as understanding the value of honesty, truth-telling, and harmonious human connections. Without such a value system, accountability and building bridges are not possible.

I have drawn strategies for the prevention of violence from what I have learned about violent, about why people don't become violent when they have risks to do, and from what I have learned about accountability. Children require long-term relationships with people who love them, who are there for them, and who show them how to form secure relationships with others. They require value systems, social skills, and vocational skills. Many people have the good fortune to be members of families and communities where these advantages are a given. Many others grow up believing that you take what you want from whomever you want and you do not owe anyone anything. That belief and value system is the bedrock of the development and commission of violent behaviors.

References

Athens, Lonnie (1997). *Violent criminal acts and actors revisited*. Urbana and Chicago: University of Illinois.

Athens, Lonnie (1992). *The creation of dangerous, violent criminals*. Urbana: University of Illinois Press.

Gilgun, Jane F. (2008b). Lived experience, reflexivity, and research on perpetrators of interpersonal violence. *Qualitative Social Work, 7(2)*, 181-197.

Gilgun, Jane F. & Alankaar Sharma (2011). The uses of humour in case management with high risk Children & their families, *British Journal of Social Work*, 1-18.

Katz, Jack (1988). *The seductions of crime*. New York: Basic.

Lawson, Louanne (2003). Isolation, gratification, justification: Offenders' explanations of child molesting. *Issues in Mental Health Nursing, 24*, 695-705.

Jane Gilgun
October 6, 2012
Minneapolis, Minnesota, USA

Contents

Part 1: The Meanings of Violence to Perpetrators

1. Do Unto Others: The Logic of Murderous Rampages — 1
2. Violence as Fun — 7
3. Why They Do It: Beliefs & Emotional Gratification Lead to Violent Acts — 14
4. Chills, Thrills, Power, & Control: The Meanings of Violence to Perpetrators — 25
5. Bobby and the Drug Store Robbery — 51
6. What Child Sexual Abuse Means to Abusers — 60
7. What Child Sexual Abuse Means to Women and Girl Perpetrators — 79
8. The Thin Blue Line of Police Brutality — 88
9. When Cops are Criminals — 92
10. The Bishop Has No Shame — 97

Part 2: The Development of Violent Behaviors

11. Two Boys, Similar Backgrounds: One Goes To Prisons and one Does Not: Why? — 101
12. Tony's Pathway to Juvenile Detention — 106
13. Jacinta's Lament: Happy Father's Day, Dad — 112

14. Pete's Pathway to Proscial Behaviors ... 130

15: Phil's Pathway to Prosocial Adult Behaviors ... 135

16. Do Sexually Abused Children Become Abusers? ... 142

17. Protective Factors, Resilience, and Child Abuse and Neglect ... 151

PART 3: ACCOUNTABILITY

18. Evil Feels Good: Think Before You Act ... 161

19. It's Time for the Roman Catholic Church to Show the World What Penitence is ... 165

20. Did Something Wrong? Admit it and Take the Consequences ... 179

21. How to Tell the Difference Between Fake Accountability and True ... 186

22. A Loving Act that Results in Harm: A Review of Sarah's Key, a Film ... 191

PART 4: THE PREVENTION OF VIOLENT BEHAVIORS

23. How to Teach Children to be Violent Offenders ... 197

24. The Prevention of Sexually Abusive Behaviors ... 201

25. Three Principles for the Prevention of Sexually Abusive Behaviors and Sexual Assault ... 220

26. Lust, Agape, Philia, and Erotic Love: Meanings in Personal Relationships ... 232

Acknowledgements ... 241

About the Author ... 242

1

Do Unto Others:
The Logic of Murderous Rampages

Why did he do it? In his own mind, Omar Thornton and other men who go on rampages did to others what he believed had been done to him. He experienced hurt beyond his capacity for reason. He hurt back. This article is a case study of Omar Thornton who killed colleagues at his workplace in August 2010. What I say about Omar fits many other men who go on murderous rampages.

He snapped, so he did, when he learned his company planned to fire him based upon a video that showed him stealing beer at work. He was a driver for a beer distributing company. He retrieved two handguns he had hidden in the company kitchen and shot and killed his supervisor and seven others. He called his mother to say goodbye. He asked her to tell "everybody" he loved them. Then he shot himself dead.

This is a 34 year-old man with a clean record and who worked long hours. Relatives and friends described him as a good person. They also said he had complained of racial harassment at work. Company spokespersons had no official record of his complaints. His name was Omar Thornton.

Complex Automatic Emotions

Shamed and enraged, Omar experienced thoughts and emotion that arose so powerfully that they overwhelmed his common sense and decency. He reverted to blueprints for action etched in his brain, laid down over the years through hard times whose meanings he shared with no one: experiences of racism, discrimination, lack of opportunity, bankruptcy, hounding of creditors, and difficulty with intimate relationships.

is many who ask, "How could someone do this? Why did y do this?" It's time to stop asking questions like these and e actions that prevent such horrific events.

y Did He Do It?

Too many risks and not enough within him to offset the s--that's why he did it. The main risk he had was his belief his fears were unshareable. He thought that if he shared n, he would be less than a man. No one showed him that it s a real man to share his deepest fears.

What can we do as individuals and as a society to create litions where children grow up willing to talk to trusted rs about their deepest fears? What can we do to show them vay out when they believe they are boxed in with no exit?

"I am hurt. I feel inadequate. No one respects me. I'm ood." These words are a start. Many people, especially men, ld rather die than say them. We have to figure out a way for and men to realize that real men own up to their feelings natter what the feelings are. Real men find someone they to talk to.

Real men know that if they don't deal with their ions they may hurt someone. Real men protect others. do not hurt others, no matter how much they hurt and no er how much they think other people are laughing at them.

We can teach boys and girls to own up to their feelings o talk to someone they trust. Boys and men especially need iow that real men face their feelings and deal with them. are not ashamed of their feelings. These ideas are very ent from what most boys and men believe.

When real men and women do something wrong, they 'I did it. I was wrong. I'm sorry. How can I make up for ' Simple words. These words need to be etched into brains lace images of shooting your way out of trouble.

We can teach children and encourage each other to say words each time they do anything wrong. Eventually such s could be as automatic as pulling out a gun and killing e. We need to learn to say these words, even when we e that others are treating us unfairly, as Omar did and as so other mass murderers do.

Blueprints for Honesty

Many people believe others treat them unfairly and the deck is stacked against them. Often, this is so. As a society, we have to decide what to do about unfair treatment on a personal level and through policies and practices. We must figure out what to do so that fewer people have blueprints etched in their brains that tell them that

1. the odds are against them and

2. when they get to a point where they see no exit, they must do whatever it takes to right the balance of the injustice they have experienced.

These blueprints tell them they must give as they have gotten. What can we do about these blueprints?

We must replace these blueprints with blueprints of honesty. We have to teach and show boys and men that real men express their deepest fears and deal with them constructively. That takes guts. Only real men can do that. We have to do all we can to make sure that constructive actions of expressing fears to trusted others is the action etched in brains when we feel hurt, enraged, and vengeful.

The Dead

Omar S. Thornton was 34 years old and grew up in Hartford, Connecticut. He killed Victor James, Craig Pepin, Bryan Cirigliano, Louis Felder, Francis Fazio Jr., Doug Scruton, Edward Kennison, and William Ackerman. These men leave shocked and grieving families and friends. Lost lives and tragedy result when we fail to replace blueprints of violence with blueprints of accountability.

Craig Pepin, Hero

Craig Pepin was a hero. He shouted to co-workers to listen to him if that were the last thing they would ever do. "There's a shooter. Get out!" he roared. He stayed behind to make sure everyone got out. Thornton shot and killed him. He may have lived had he been less concerned about others. This is a real man.

Thornton walked by a woman in a wheelchair. She did not know why he spared her. His blueprint for action must not have included killing people with obvious disabilities.

As Was Done to You

In his own mind, Omar Thornton and other men who go on rampages did to others what he believed had been done to him. He experienced hurt beyond his capacity for reason. He hurt back. Is this what we want?

References

14 dead, 50 wounded in shooting at Colorado theater, police chief says (2012). CNN US, July 20. http://articles.cnn.com/2012-07-20/us/us_colorado-theater-shooting_1_gunshot-wounds-gunman-theater

Connecticut shooting horror (2010). New York Post. August 4. http://www.nypost.com/f/mobile/news/local/connecticut_shooting_horror_mjGpPhDo2vxzvfS9RVkmwM

Gilgun, Jane F. (2011). Evil feels good: Think before you act. Chapter in present book. http://www.amazon.com/s/ref=nb_sb_noss?url=search-alias%3Daps&field-keywords=Jane+Gilgun+evil+feels+good

2

Violence as Fun

Deryl Dedmon and his friends were out to have a little fun. For about a month, this group of young men hunted down black men to harass. Their last bit of fun ended in murder when Mr. Dedmon ran over James Anderson who was lying in a parking lot after the young men had beaten him.

Once again young white men harassed and killed a man of color, this time in Jackson, Mississippi. A group of young men in two vehicles drove 18 miles to find African American men to harass. They sought men who were homeless or drunk because they thought such men would be unlikely to report the harassment to police. The first black man they found was James Anderson, 47, who was standing by his car in a motel parking lot early one morning last June. Some of the teenagers jumped out of the vehicles and punched Mr. Anderson. As Mr. Anderson stumbled, Deryl Dedmon, 19, accelerated his truck and ran over Mr. Anderson and killed him.

The teenagers shouted "white power" during the assault. Later, Mr. Dedmon bragged on his cell phone about how he had just run over a black man, whom he described with a racial epithet. The murder of Mr. Anderson came at the end of a month-long series of assaults that these young men committed against black men.

In March 2012, Mr. Dedmon, was sentenced to life in prison and now faces federal charges. "I wish I could take it all back," Mr. Dedmon said. "I was young and dumb, ignorant and full of hatred. I chose to go down the wrong path."

Jail-House Conversion

Mr. Dedmon experienced a jail-house conversion. He asked Mr. Anderson's family for forgiveness. He said, "As I stand before you today, I am a changed man. I am a godly man.

God has showed me to see no colors. God showed me that we are all made in the image of God so we are all based on the same thing," he said. "I do not ask y'all to forget, but I do ask y'all to forgive."

It's too late. James Anderson is dead. Dedmon ran him over with his truck to have a little fun. The deed is done.

Thomas E. Perez said in a statement, "This is really a case about a group of racist thugs who made a sport of targeting vulnerable African Americans in Jackson and attacking them without provocation simply because of the color of their skin." Mr. Perez is the assistant attorney general for the U.S. Justice Department's civil rights division. He continued, "On a number of occasions they drove around Jackson looking for African-Americans to assault. Jackson is a venerable community, however, for these defendants Jackson was 'Jafrica' [and] African Americans were subhuman."

Predictable

This situation is similar to many others that occur in the United States each year. Young white men, seeking excitement, want to be part of a group of young men who assert themselves as men, seek a man or men of color to harass. This is their idea of fun. This is a bonding experience. This is what men do to show they are men, at least in their own minds. For such men, violence is exciting and a high. They target men who are members of minority groups, and they yuck it up.

In the murder of James Anderson, the teenagers asserted "white power." Not only white power, but white **men's** power over black men. They were so into asserting themselves as white men having power over black men that they didn't think about fairness, and they didn't think about consequences for themselves and for Mr. Anderson. They didn't think about consequences for those who loved them—their own families and friends. They didn't think about consequences for the friends and families of Mr. Jackson. They were oblivious to the fears that their behaviors evoke in the parents of young black men and the fears their behaviors evoke for the safety of all black men—and other males of color.

Any moral values, any family values, any sense of fairness that they might have had were not in play.

Cowardice, Not Power

White power? What they did is not an assertion of power of any kind. It's an assertion of predatory, aggressive group behavior against a single black man. They sought black men in vulnerable situations. That's cowardice, besides being predatory behavior. A group of young men, so numerous that they needed two vehicles, attack a lone black man. That is ganging up. Mr. Anderson had no chance to defend himself against a group of men.

To gang up on someone in not power but it is cowardice and predatory aggression. Mr. Anderson was in a vulnerable situation, alone in a parking lot early on a June morning. The power these men asserted was an abuse of power. They sought and took advantage of a lone black man for their own gratification, sense of belonging, and affirmation of their identity as real men, as real white men.

It's cowardice for another reason. These teen boys set out to find a drunk or homeless black man. They deliberately sought not only persons vulnerable because they were alone, but vulnerable because they were incapacitated through drunkenness or stigmatized and powerless because of homelessness. There was no way these young white men could lose in the scenarios they sought. That's the very definition of predatory behavior and cowardice.

Race-Based Hate

It was white, all right, but it was not power. It was abuse of power that these white men asserted. These were white teenage males acting out against a black man. They must have conjured up in their minds that this lone black man did something to deserve to be harassed and then run over. What did he do? He existed. That's all he did. Mr. Anderson was a black man who was alive. He had the misfortune to be in the wrong place at the wrong time, at precisely the time that a group of young white men were looking for black men to harass.

Not Lone Wolves

The teenagers were men seeking to prove they were men, bonding in acts of violence in ways that for some men are rituals and rites of passage in the United States today. Young men who act this way are not lone wolves: they believe what many other men believe. Some women probably believe the same things, too. To hunt in packs is manly, like lions, jackals, and wolves who look for isolated cloven hoofed animals to bring down and devour.

The thinking of these young white men is a pattern of wide-spread beliefs: Violence is fun, being part of a group of real men is fun, white men are superior to all others, and race-based hatred is justified, and a persons' race justifies violence against them. Being white, male, and violent toward black men are opportunities for bonding experiences for far too many white men, young or otherwise.

Where do These Ideas Come From?

The men are not lone wolves, but part of a large group of men who have committed similar acts of violence and part of an even larger group of men who think the way they do. These men share beliefs about themselves as white men, about how to act toward men who are members of races that are not white, about violence as fun and justifiable in many situations, and about bonding and belonging with other white men. They are the "in" group. Men of other races are the "out" group. They decide who is in and who is out. They act on their beliefs. They celebrate their solidarity and belonging through violence against those who are in the out group.

Men who act this way learned these beliefs. They also learned that real men not only share these beliefs, but they sometimes have to act on these beliefs to prove that they are real men. If they don't act, they are not be real men. They are vulnerable to accusations that they are chicken, don't have the guts. They seek the rewards not only of saying they have these beliefs but also of acting upon them.

There are gains in these beliefs. Men who have these beliefs feel good about themselves. They feel validated. They count. They are part of a brotherhood of real men, whom they define as white men. Their self-respect depends upon being part of a group who believes these things. Their identities as men depends upon beliefs.

There are losses in these beliefs as well. Strangely, people who hold these beliefs do not think of the losses until it is too late. Deryl Redmon understood the losses, after he was sentenced to life in prison for the murder of James Anderson.

I once asked a man who raped if he thought about what might happen to him before he committed a rape. He said, "Rape is worth giving up a bundle for." At 19, he was in prison for the next 12 years for rape.

Self-Interest?

You would think self-interest would stop the kinds of acts that Mr. Redmon, his friends, and so many others commit. Maybe they don't think about what will happen to them if they are caught. They might think they will get away with it. Many people do. They might dismiss the impact of consequences. I doubt they think the consequences are worth it once the consequences smack them up. They obviously don't think about the consequences for the people they harm. They might, however, anticipate their own joy at seeing the suffering they cause, at least at the moment they are doing harm.

Christian Values?

Ironically, many of the white men who harass and are violent against men of color are Christians, where the central commandment is to love the Lord our God with all our hearts and minds and to love our neighbors as ourselves. Their beliefs about being white, being male, being superior to others, violence as sporting good fun, and members of other races as deserving of bad treatment over-rides their family values, their Christian values. These beliefs are more powerful than common decency, common sense, self-interest, family values, and Christian values.

Discussion

Many people believe what these young men believed as they hunted for a black man to harass, found James Anderson, ganged up on him, punched him, ran him over, killed him, and called him racial epithets after he was dead—and had a hell of a time doing these things. It's time to challenge these belief systems. It's time to ask how they can be so stupid. Such cowards? How can they act against their own self interest? Is being part of a group of real white men that important? Is asserting your own white male superiority that important? Is betraying your own Christian values that important?

The same questions apply to people who harass and kill lesbians, gays, bisexuals, transgender persons, to men who beat, rape, and murder women, and to men who are violent against others because of their religious beliefs. No one can answer these questions for other people. People who have these beliefs have to ask themselves what matters to them—and what price they are willing to pay for acting on these beliefs.

Note: The day after Mr. Redmon's conviction on state charges, he pled guilty to federal hate crime charges. He will serve 50 years in federal prison and then serve his life sentence in state prison. Two of Mr. Redmon's friends also pled guilty to federal hate crime charges. Mr. Redmon could have received the death penalty, but Mr. Anderson's family asked for clemency.

References

Gilgun, Jane F. (2010). Evil feels good: Think before you act. Chapter in present book. http://www.amazon.com/s/ref=nb_sb_noss?url=search-alias%3Daps&field-keywords=Jane+Gilgun+evil+feels+good

Gilgun, Jane F. (2011). Why they do it: Beliefs and emotional gratification lead to violent acts. Chapter in present book. http://www.amazon.com/s/ref=nb_sb_noss?url=search-alias%3Daps&field-keywords=Jane+Gilgun+why+they+do+it

Prince, Zanitha (2012). Miss. white men plead guilty to hate-fueled killing of James Anderson. *Seattle Medium*, March 28.

http://www.seattlemedium.com/News/search/ArchiveContent.asp?NewsID=113048&sID=

Severson, Kim (2012). Three plead guilty to hate crimes in the killing of black man in Mississippi. *New York Times*, March 23, A17.

Severson, Kim (2012). White teenager who drove over and killed black man is sentenced to life. *New York Times*, March 22, A13.

3

Why They Do It: Beliefs & Emotional Gratification Lead to Violent Acts

Desire for vengeance and fun are two reasons people commit violent acts. In this essay, I use several different cases to show that beliefs and desires for emotional gratification lead to decisions to commit violence. I first present the general features of why people kill and do other violent things such as rape and physical violence. Then I show how these general features can be used to understand individual cases.

People commit violent acts because of their beliefs. They also almost always get a strong emotional charge out of being violent. These two features are the core of why people are violent: Beliefs and emotional charge. There are many variations after that, but these are the constants.

Beliefs

Violent people build an image of their victims in their minds. They decide who the victims are and then act on their beliefs. Who the victims think they are and who other people believe the victims are do not matter. All that matters to perpetrators is who they think the victims are.

Don

A graduate of an elite private college, Don decided the women he raped were "loose" and out looking for sex anyway. So, it was no big thing when he followed them home in the dark and raped them. This is the conversation I had with him when I interviewed him in a maximum security prison where he lived for 17 years for his rape convictions.

> Um, and if I take the right person, you know, it's not going to make a difference anyway. You know, because, like I said before, you know, the women I was, was raping were, you know, they'd been in that bar looking for guys anyway....You know, all my victims were, you know, they, my set up was that they'd been out in bars or loose sexually, kinds of people. So they had it coming, or they, you know, it didn't matter to them. So, so, you know, this wouldn't be a big, big thing to happen to them.

After Don's statement that rape would not be "a big, big thing" to the women, I was speechless for 20 seconds. When I finally was able to speak, I asked Don how he knew the women were loose. His answer revealed more of his thinking:

> J: (10 sec) Yeah. (10 sec) Well, how did you know that they were at bars and were loose? What...[interrupted].
> D: Well, I mean, I didn't actually know that.
> J: Oh.
> D: I, I knew, I knew that because that's the kind of people that were out at that time of night.
> J: Okay. So you would be looking at what time of night?
> D: Yeah.
> J: What, what time of night would you be out?
> D: Well, generally the, and this, this is another thing that doesn't make sense because there was all kinds of times that I was out.
> J: Oh.
> D: But, generally it would be late, like you know, midnight, one o'clock, two o'clock in the morning, that kind of thing. But you know I was out in, in the winter time sometimes after it got dark, you know, o not right after it got dark but maybe at seven-thirty or eight o'clock, or something.

Don decided that some women deserved to be raped and he acted on his beliefs. He was unable to step outside of his own frame of reference.

I saw this inability to step outside of a frame of reference repeatedly in research I did with about 150 men or so who had committed violent acts. They are oblivious to the idea that other people have dignity and worth and have the right to make their own decisions. Fairness and caring are not part of their constructions of others.

Harley

Don did not have personal relationships with the women he raped, but Harley only beat his wives and girlfriends. He beat them when he thought they disrespected them. Whether their actions showed disrespect is a matter of dispute. How he defined them and their behaviors is what lead to his actions. This is an example of Harley's beliefs.

> I brutally beat up one of my girlfriends one time because we had moved to this house. She had asked me to clean up the house. Vacuum the rugs is what it was because she wanted to put the furniture in, mop the floor. I went and got drunk. I came back. She asked me this at twelve o'clock. I came back in the house at nine-thirty. She had mopped the house and straightened the house up. The house looked good. I jumped on her and beat her up.
> In my mind, she was trying to make me look like an ass because she could have waited on me to clean up, to do this. She asked me to do it. I mean I just didn't only beat her up. I mean I knocked out all the windows in the house with my fist. I mean I'm standing here bleeding, my fingers, all these cuts and stuff like this on my hands. I'm standing there bleeding. She's bleeding. I mean I've beaten her so bad. I couldn't beat her any more. I knocked out all the windows. I just was a raging lunatic.

Harley elaborated on his beliefs.

> My first wife, I used to just beat her so bad, just turn the house up side down and just beat her. For what reason? She may have asked me a question, asked me, why did I go to work that day. Any kind of question that

doesn't sit with me turns into violence. I could always take it and turn whatever they said into the way I wanted it to be. What are you trying to do? You're trying to shame me. You're trying to embarrass me. You're not giving me any respect. Those are my famous words: 'I'm a grown man. I deserve my respect. I want my respect. You don't come in, and you don't try to tell me what to do.'

Cory

Besides beliefs about women, what it means to be a man, and the right to construct others as they see fit, many perpetrators also believe that if they are hurting enough they have the right to hurt others. Cory raped and beat his wife in front of their three year-old daughter because he was convinced his wife had cheated on him. Many men believe that if wives cheat, men have to punish them and re-establish themselves as men. This is how Cory described his hurt and what he does with it.

When somebody's done something or what not, I'll say to myself, I'll use my exact words. 'You fucking dickhead, you have no idea of who you're even saying that to. I'll rip your skull off.' That sense of power is inside of me. It's always there, that sense of power, how powerful you are. Okay? I go, 'Listen to you.' That will be my exact words. 'If you only knew. If you only knew.'

This is weird about me. All right? I see myself with this great big heart. Okay? Picture this. This heart in me is this big. (He holds his hands about two feet apart.) At times when somebody comes up and tries to poke that heart that I get relatively mad. Okay? Then sometimes when that heart actually gets punctured then I get angry and rageful. Okay? In most cases in my life, I think, the person that got hurt was me. There were times when I got tired of hurting me and I want somebody else to pay. Like the time I beat my wife.

Emotional Gratification

These three men described the emotional gratification they experienced when they were violent toward others.

Don

Almost all of the perpetrators I interviewed enjoyed themselves while they were being violent. Don, discussed earlier, was a high school football player. He described the physical experience of anticipating his rapes.

> Well, nothing, nothing ever gave me the intense kind of feeling. Especially the, there would be, like, like when I was driving around and I would be thinking about it, maybe following somebody, I had, you know, like a physical reaction. I would be shaking, physically shaking, like teeth would chatter, and I couldn't stop. You know, it wouldn't stop, and I never had that kind of, you know, physical reaction to, to anything else. I would also get, you know, like butterflies and I can, you know, relate that to, you know, sports events, you know, before a big game or something. You know, that feeling but not the, not the physical [meaning, he didn't have an erection before a big game, but did when he was driving around looking for a woman alone after dark in her car].

Anticipating rape inflamed Don. His behavior evoked images of man the hunter, man the questor, man the predator, man the sports hero. This also is showing himself as a real man. For Don, the audience is himself and perhaps an imaginary audience who believed, as he told me he did, that real men have sex whenever they want. He was living up to his ideal of man the sexual conqueror who has sex with whomever he chooses whenever he wants.

Harley

Like many other perpetrators, Harley enjoyed himself as he behaved in violent ways.

I actually had these people afraid. My family's afraid. The people outside my family's afraid. Friends of my family's afraid. My sister's girlfriend, her and her husband came over to the house one night. Her husband, like we got into an argument. I jumped up, and I grabbed him, slammed him up against the wall. Here's my sister crying. Here's this guy's wife--she's crying. I'm like, what are these people crying about? They're giving me this high, this, this feeling of control or power.

I got power now over these people. They're telling me, "Oh don't hurt him. Don't hurt him." My sister, she said, "You don't know my brother. Control yourself. He might kill him." I've got this power. I love that. I love people to dress me up.

Cory

Cory also enjoyed his violence. I could see that as he described what happened when somebody pricked what he called his great big heart: "You have no idea who you're dealing with." He thought beating his wife would help him feel better about his conviction that she had cheated on him. He told me

That night I said to myself, If you go over there and do this you're going to feel better afterwards, you know. I'm going to make you pay for hurting me. This is the last time you're going to hurt me.

In acts of physical violence with other men, his wounds were badges of manhood. He said

I've woken up in the morning with this lip hanging out here, eyes swollen shut, and my nose broken. I had my friends come over. We yucked it up about it. 'Ha, ha. That was a hell of a fight, wasn't it?' Somehow I was a man then.

Same Patterns, Different Cases

I saw these patterns repeatedly in my interviews with men who had committed violent acts: beliefs and emotional gratification. In media reports of violence, these same features show up repeatedly. A few examples, some of them old, show what I mean. A witness to the school murders in Littleton, Colorado, said "every time they'd shoot someone, they'd holler, like it was, like, exciting."

Another student reported, "They were laughing after they shot. It was like they were having the time of their lives." In 1996, 14 year-old Barry Loukatis, killed a boy who had teased him. He also killed two other boys. He said "It sure beats algebra, doesn't it?' as he stood over a dying boy who was choking on his own blood. This was 16 years ago. Times have not changed.

Murder of Children in China

In late spring 2010, four men in China in separate incidents assaulted and killed preschool children and children in primary schools. Because guns are unavailable in China, three men used knives and one a hammer. Almost 60 children were injured and eight additional children died. Had the assailants used guns, many more children and adults would have died. In the latest attack, on the last day of April, teachers pulled two children from the attackers arms as he prepared to light himself on fire. He died in the fire.

Newspaper articles quoted Chinese citizens who can't understand why this is happening. The article also provided several theories. The men are unemployed and are taking their frustration out on children. "Children are the one people care about the most, and they are the most innocent," said a sociology professor at a Chinese university. Some speculated that these are copycat killings, given the publicity about them. Finally, there are thoughts that the men are mentally ill, which led to expressions of concerns about China's lack of mental health services.

None of these theories mentioned beliefs and none mentioned the emotional gratification the men may have experienced as they planned and then acted on their violence.

Beliefs are likely to have had a lot to do with these attacks on children. All four perpetrators were men. It is likely that they interpreted their circumstances in terms of their masculinity. The gap between what they thought they should achieve and what they actually achieved may have been impossible for them to handle. Their unemployment may have convinced them they were unworthy of respect.

They may have become alienated from friends and family rather than seeking comfort from them. Their beliefs about masculinity may have led them to believe that they would be seen as even less worthy of respect as men, as being weak, if they admitted to others how upset and hurt they were. Under no circumstances could they risk seeing themselves as weak, or having others see them that way.

Thus, they probably were hurting badly, based upon their beliefs. Like Cory, they may have wanted others to hurt as badly as they did. They may have chosen young children as victims because they knew this would hurt other people badly. Hurting adults is not as big a hurt as harming children.

They also may have felt like nobodies. When they saw other men get noticed when they harmed children may have given them ideas about how others would know who they are.

The one man who killed himself may have felt so much intense hurt—the kind of hurt that Cory described—that his only way out was to set himself on fire. His attempt to take two children with him suggests that he was dead serious about hurting others as he was hurt.

Newspaper accounts do not state what the demeanors of the men were, but based on my research, I believe that they felt their spirits lifting when they planned their crimes as they committed their crimes. Violence helped them feel better, too, just as others I've quoted and so many other cases show.

Mental illness is a popular explanation for why people commit such violent acts. This does not hold water because most people who have mental illnesses are not violent, just as most people who do not have mental illnesses are not violent. People with mental illnesses who are violent have beliefs that violence is what you are supposed to do under certain prescribed circumstances. People with mental illnesses and who are violent have the same beliefs as people without mental illness and who are violent.

Murder in Minneapolis

After Trace Maxwell killed his girlfriend and two men, he led police on a slow chase down city streets until he shot and killed himself in late April 2010. Newspaper reports give few details about what was going on in Trace's mind. He obviously thought murder and suicide would solve whatever what bothering him. He also shot his girlfriend's roommate. She survived.

Trace appeared to have believed his girlfriend had cheated on him. Like Cory and Harley, his solution was violence. Somehow his manhood was disrespected, and he was going to set her straight. He believed the two men had cheated him out of money. Trace was, among other things, a drug dealer and pimp who had been in prison. If he were a real man, he could not let these men get away with cheating him. His friends said he killed himself because he did not want to go back to prison.

That might be so, but down deep, he may have believed that as a grown man, no one could tell him what to do, including ordering him to prison for three murders and one attempted murder. He was going to get away with it, and he was going to be in control of his life, even if it meant ending his life.

Trace had a hair-trigger temper, often "going off" on people. His long record of police involvement shows a pattern of not controlling this emotional responses. A technical term for his "temper" is "reactivity." Trace apparently had a highly reactive way of dealing with things that displeased him. Such reactivity probably served him well. He got what he wanted through intimidation and threats. A lot of people are like this. Many of their highly reactive responses are related to unresolved traumas, such as abuse and neglect in childhood, witnessing violence, bullying, losses, thinking that's what you are supposed to do, and the like. On the other hand, this reactivity is often instrumental. It gets people what they want. Intimidation works much of the time.

Any one or several of these factors may have been true for Trace as well. Yet, most highly reactive people do not murder others and most do not hurt others. They may hurt themselves through cutting themselves, overeating, or drinking too much alcohol, or they may deal constructively with their strong emotional reactions. Very few murder, rape, beat others up, or even verbally abuse others.

Beliefs as Core

With Trace, then, the core issue is beliefs about what he is entitled to do when he is upset with others. Murder them—that is what he believed. When other people are closing in on him, don't let that happen. Kill yourself. These are beliefs. When people don't do what you want, intimidate them. Murder them if you have to.

Newspaper accounts do not have information about whether Trace felt gratified as he planned and executed his shootings and murders, but he must have. The satisfaction of doing exactly what you want is gratifying. The satisfaction of foiling police in not allowing them to take him alive must have been gratifying. His last thought could have been, They're not going to take me alive. How gratifying. How short-sighted.

Discussion

It's time to stop wondering why they do it. They do it because they believe violence is what they are supposed to do. Violence gets them what they want. A web of beliefs comes together when people commit violent acts. The anticipation of gratification at committing violence and the gratification of actually doing the violence overcome any thoughts that such acts are not a good idea. Having your own way is central.

It's time to think about what each of us can do to unravel beliefs that lead to violent acts.

References

5 Chinese kids hurt in new attack (2010). *Minneapolis Star Tribune.* May 1, 2010. p. A6.

Gilgun, Jane F. (2010). *Child sexual abuse: From harsh realities to hope.* Amazon Kindle, & Nook.

Gilgun, Jane F. (2010). *The NEATS: A child and family assessment.* Amazon Kindle, & Nook.

Gilgun, Jane F. (2008). Lived experience, reflexivity, and research on perpetrators of interpersonal violence. *Qualitative Social Work, 7(2),* 181-197.

Gilgun, Jane F. (1999). Fingernails painted red: A feminist, semiotic analysis of "hot" text, *Qualitative Inquiry, 5,* 181-207.

Gilgun, Jane F. (2006). Children and adolescents with problematic sexual behaviors: Lessons from research on resilience. In Robert Longo & Dave Prescott (Eds*.), Current perspectives on working with sexually aggressive youth and youth with sexual behavior problems* (pp. 383-394). Holyoke, MA: Neari Press.

Gilgun, Jane F., & Laura S. Abrams (2005). Gendered adaptations, resilience, and the perpetration of violence. In Michael Ungar (Ed*.), Handbook for working with children and Youth: Pathways to resilience across cultures and context* (pp. 57-70). Toronto: University of Toronto Press

Gilgun, Jane F., Danette Jones, & Kay Rice. (2005). Emotional expressiveness as an indicator of progress in treatment. In Martin C. Calder (Ed.), *Emerging approaches to work with children and young people who sexually abuse* (pp. 231-244). Dorset, England: Russell House.

Gilgun, Jane F., & Laura McLeod (1999). Gendering violence. *Studies in Symbolic Interactionism, 22,* 167-193.

Gilgun, Jane F. (1996). Human development and adversity in ecological perspective, Part 2: Three patterns. *Families in Society, 77,* 459-576. Gilgun, Jane F. (1996). Human development and adversity in ecological perspective: Part 1: A conceptual framework. *Families in Society, 77,* 395-402.

Gilgun, Jane F. (1995). We shared something special: The moral discourse of incest perpetrators. *Journal of Marriage and the Family, 57,* 265-281.

McKinney, Matt, Joy Powell, & David Chanen (2010). Hints of motives appear in Twin Cities slaying rampage. *Minneapolis Star Tribune.* May 1, 2010. A1, A7.

Sharma, Alankaar & Jane F. Gilgun (2008). What perpetrators say about child sexual abuse. *Indian Journal of Social Work, 69(3),* 321-338.

4

Chills, Thrills, Power, & Control
The Meanings of Violence
to Perpetrators
1996

This is part of a paper I wrote in 1966 for a conference. In it, I show the many different meanings. I could not figure out how to write this paper as a journal article, but I did use parts of it in a book chapter (Gilgun, 2002). The reason that I didn't try to publish it is because I didn't know how to fit what I have learned into traditional journal formats. I am now ready to write the ideas of this paper up for a journal. I think I know how to do it, more than 16 years later. I wrote the paper for the Preconference Workshop on Theory Development and Research Methodology, the National Council on Family Relations, Kansas City, Missouri, USA, November 5, 1996.

I have identified several dimensions of violence through 10 years of in-depth life history, phenomenological interviewing of about 65 persons, mostly men and most of whom have committed violent acts. The average number of interviews is about 12, but ranges from one to about 30. Not only do I do life histories in domains such as family history and relationships, history of peer relationships, relationships with extended family and persons in community settings such as schools and neighborhoods, sexual development, and history of violent behaviors, but I obtain detailed accounts of violent acts they've committed. A thorough presentation of my method is in Gilgun (in press).

In discussing the phenomenological dimensions of violence, I am using the following approaches: First, I presented the categories of the dimensions of violence and illustrated these dimensions with quotes that show that aspects of the experience of violence can be categorized as I have categorized them.
Then, I illustrated how most if not all of these dimensions of violence play themselves out in one individual case. I boldface

and italicize the terms designating the categories each time I use them. Finally, I tried to show that these dimensions are present in popular literature, such as contemporary murder mysteries, trade books, and in some newspaper articles. I've found it much harder to identify scholarly sources that look at the subjective dimensions of violence.

The Dimensions

Through 10 years of interviewing persons who have acted in violent ways, I have discovered that violence as experienced by perpetrators has several dimensions: gratification, vengeance, entitlement, proving you've got guts, expediency, self-protection, and protecting others. Interlacing each of these dimensions is the experience of having power over others, which, for those who are violent, usually is gratifying and sometimes exhilarating. Being able to control others is part of some but not all of these dimensions, and perpetrators often experience control as gratifying and exhilarating as well. Sometimes persons who are committing violent acts experience fear as well, which they attempt to overcome in order to achieve what instrumental and/or affective end they are seeking through their acts of violence.

Gratification

The term *gratification* actually is a proxy for all the pleasurable, pleasing, thrilling, exhilarating feelings that perpetrators have when they commit violent acts. I've found that many of my informants experience a tremendous high through violence. These powerfully positive feelings range from intense feelings of love that incest perpetrators sometimes feel for their victims (see Gilgun, 1995a for many examples), to intense pleasure in "getting over on other people"--the joy of "I've won," to the bone-shaking thrill of the hunt. Occasionally, however, some violent persons experience little subjective pleasure. In the space I have, I can only illustrate some of the themes related to gratification.

Sexually Abusing Children

One man who raped girlfriends, wives, and strangers, also sexually abused children. He said about his sexual abuse of children, "It was warm, comfortable, gentle, you know. It was like making love."

A Rapist Stalking a Victim

The following quote is from a well-educated man from an upper middle class background who was convicted of seven rapes that he committed while engaged to be married and sexually active with his fiancée.

> Well, nothing, nothing ever gave me the intense kind of feeling. Especially the, there would be, like, like when I was driving around and I would be thinking about it, maybe following somebody, I had you know like a physical reaction, I would be shaking, physically shaking, like teeth would chatter, and I couldn't stop, you know it wouldn't stop. And I never had that kind of you know physical reaction to, to anything else. I would also get, you know like butterflies and I can, you know, relate that to you know sports events, you know before a big game or something. You know that feeling but not the, not the physical. (Note: I used this quote in McLeod & Gilgun, 1995.)

The Thrill of Burglary

How burglars experience burglary is very different from everyday thinking. One man, a drug addict, loved burglary. Once he got into a house, he said, "It was like Christmas...Sometimes I got so excited I had to have a bowel movement." Another burglar, who also was a drug addict, eroticized invading other people's private space.

He said:

> Part of the excitement was going through the drawers, looking through their panties and their bras, and looking through their private things. You know, it was like it's not private anymore because I know about it. I had a real, real powerful sense about that.

The Thrill of People "Dressing Me Up"

This man quoted here has a long history of physical assault, including three convictions a three different time for the attempted murder of three different girlfriends. He loved seeing other people's fear of him. Forthcoming about the subjective experience of his violence, he also had more distanced, cognitive labels for his experiences: power and control.

> My family's afraid. You know, the people outside my family's afraid. Friends of my family's afraid, you know. Ah, ah, my sister's girlfriend, her and her husband came over one, to the house one night, and, ah, her, ah, her husband, like we got into an argument, you know, and I jumped up, you know, and I grabbed him, slammed him up against the wall, and you know, like, then my sis, here's my sister crying. Here's her, here's this guy's husband, ah wife, this guy's wife, she's crying, you know, and the people in the house are like, you know, I'm like, 'What are these people crying about?' You know. Then, but they're giving me this high, this, this feeling of control or power....I got power now over these people. Look, you know, and they telling me, 'Oh, don't hurt him. Don't hurt him.' My sister she said, 'Oh, you don't know my brother. Control yourself. He might kill him. You know, man, and, and, I've got this power. You know, and I love that. You know I love, I love people to dress me up.

The thrill, in many cases, is related to a sense of power, as in the above excerpt. Showing others he had the power to hurt someone and then scaring his audience with his power to hurt, gives him a tremendous high.

No Thrill

Occasionally, informants told me there was no pleasure in the violence. A man who robbed convenience stores he had to overcome fear and anxiety to get the money to buy drugs:

> It's not easy to go out and rob somebody....Because you always have in the back of your mind what if you get caught. What if, what if? That raised doubt.... So you, you go through all that anx, anxiety you know. Heavy anxiety too, you got to go through that stuff. I know for me, my ah, my drug habit would make me forget all about that because when I anticipate that I'm going to get high, man. I, that's what makes me deal with that anxiety. I say, 'Well, shit, well, look at the long run. I'm going to get high.'

Because of his drug addiction, this man lost a white collar job. He also was a former college star football player.

A man who killed his fiancée said

I was not angry when I killed her. I was sad. I guess I was just real depressed. I was sad, but not angry.

He also expressed no thrill, no gratification.

Power

Sometimes the power remains at the level of threat, as in a confined setting of a prison, but the pleasure of the sense of power in the threat is evident in his words. The following excerpt illustrates this. In fact, this man was in prison for a brutal assault on his wife.

> You know, occasionally, at times, I find myself, at times now, when somebody's done something around here....the unit. I'll say to myself, these are my exact words: 'Fucking dickhead, you know. You have no idea who you're even saying that to. I could rip your skull off.' That sense of power is inside of me. It's always there, okay. And that sense of power is there that says, you know, you know, how powerful you are, okay. When you feel a little bit threatened, okay, sometimes that will pop up. I go, (chuckle), 'I go, listen to you,' you know. Those will be my exact words....I have to listen to you. If you only knew. I'm sure there are guys in here who have no idea and no matter how many times I've told them or talked about it I don't think they have any idea who they're dealing with.

Another man, in and out of correctional facilities since he was 13 for sexual assault, talked about how powerful he felt in seeing his victims' fear:

> It's a, it's like a rush. It's like shooting your arm full of dope. I don't know. I never shot my arm full of dope (laugh) but I can imagine the rush you get.... It's like a total body rush.

This man did not have any audience, unlike the man who said he liked to have people "dress him up."

Control

Control appeared in many guises, such as gaining control of victims and feeling gratified by that, fighting any control that others understandably expect, and even to the point of killing someone to protect the self or others. Some of these themes are illustrated.

Protecting Others

The man who murdered his fiancée and a second woman engaged in prostitution in his apartment on the same day knew he'd go to prison for these murders. He, therefore, killed his children because he was concerned for their futures, an extreme form of control. Perhaps he saw his act as "mercy-killing," and he was trying to **protect** the children from what he was sure was a miserable future.

> Well, I killed my kids out of, ah, out of my, uh, deluded thinking of, ah, ah, a concern for their future....How will they live and who will take care of them. I can't, I can't provide for their future, and uh, I don't want them to be miserable. I don't want them bopped around in foster homes and county this or that or be abused, separated and blah blah blah you know and what will the outcome of the kids be. With all my drugged up thinking I thought they would be better off dead, you know.

Refusing Reasonable Controls

One man, a rapist, a drug addict, a drug dealer, and a burglar, responded to a question I asked about whether he'd bitten anyone. He responded

> P: Yeah, my victims. Ummm two that I know offhand. Ummm when they were, you know, they told me not to bite their nipples, and I bit their nipples.
> J: How hard?
> P: Well, I had got a reaction out of them. I probably left my mark, my teeth mark.

Entitlement

In many of the above excerpts and others in this paper, that these perpetrators experience violence as an entitlement comes through. That is, they express themselves as if they an indisputable right to beat, to rape, to take life. Often the sense of entitlement is more subtle, such as feeling entitled to define other people's meanings. Rapists, for example, often view their victims as worthy of being violated--they're tramps, they're teases, they going to do this a thousand times so what difference does forcing them make.

Perhaps the most subtle entitlement of all is the fact that these perpetrators do violence without thinking about it. The following excerpts illustrates several of these themes. The man who is speaking was a master's level social worker who was the executive director of an organization that served vulnerable adolescent boys. He molested the boy of whom he is speaking. The boy was deaf and mute and was under the agency's care. I had asked him about whether he felt vulnerable when he molested this boy.

> The kid was getting his needs met, and I was getting my needs met....We were both vulnerable. He being vulnerable to the fact that he was being molested and that he was underage and innocent, and me being vulnerable in that I was the offender and could easily be put away for life or something like that. Plus the living on the edge feeling too of, you know, what if somebody, like if I was at my office, what if the janitor came in at an odd hour and walked in on us or at least walked in, the door was locked, but walked in at the point where they might find there was something really wrong or weird was going on, or you know, just different signs that might indicate that I was doing something I shouldn't be doing. I was living, you know, there was that feeling of living on the edge of a cliff.

This man is speaking for the child, such as saying the boy was getting his needs met and was vulnerable, just as he was vulnerable. He was non-reflective about the ethics of defining the boy's experience, and certainly his lack of ethics about the molestation is obvious.

Expedience

Some informants talked about using physical force and intimidation to get control of victims. Once they had control through violence, they could proceed with the next steps in their violent acts. The rapist whose teeth would chatter and who was quoted earlier said he had sexual feelings when he thought about raping someone and was out looking for victims. When I asked him about sexual feelings during his rapes, he said

> The sexual feelings really didn't come, come back and, it's kind of, they didn't come back until, until I was in like control of the situation, and then the, you know, the, the fantasies or whatever, then, you know, when I, once I was in control of the situation, then the fantasies would come back and take over and then the, the sexual feelings would come from the fantasies.

Another man said he killed a prostitute because he did not want to pay her and didn't want any trouble about it afterward:

> I guess my solution, my solution was to kill (emphasis) her. We smoke a joint. I gave her a beer, and I'm smoking a joint, and we negotiated a price or something--50 dollars. We went it to have sex, and, uh, I think it was just intercourse, and I'm thinking I'm not going to give her 50 bucks. You know, I got 50 dollars I got about 60 dollars and I'm not giving her the last of my money. What goes through my mind is if I don't give her the money somebody is going to come around here banging on the door and all this kind of shit, and I'm not going have this bullshit, you know. I'm not going to have her boyfriends coming over here threatening me, trying to get into the apartment or something. So I just I don't really know what happened. I know what happened.... I just killed her. I just strangled her. I just, you know. I mean, it wasn't a sexual thing and just like I pulled out of her, and, uh, I decided fuck this. I'm not going to give her no money, and I'm not going have no trouble and I killed her.

Vengeance

Vengeance took many forms, that includes such categories as restoring honor, redressing a wrong, and taking out rage at someone else on a more amenable target.

Restoring Honor

Sometimes violence restores a sense of honor. One man explained his subjective experience of having his honor violated:

> I see myself as a great big heart [holds out hands to show the size of his heart, Jane, okay. Got a picture of this, the heart being this big, okay. I see times when somebody comes up and tries to poke that heart and I get relatively mad. okay. And then I feel sometimes when my heart actually gets punctured. Then I get angry and rageful. In most cases in my life, the person who got hurt is me. You know, but in other cases I got tired of hurting me and I wanted somebody else to pay, you know.

He brutally beat and raped his wife in front of his five year-old daughter, the crime for which he was convicted and for which he expressed great remorse.

Another man beat his girlfriend because she cleaned up the house after he was several hours late to help her. He felt she had insulted him.

> You know, I brutally beat up one of my girlfriends one time because, ah, we had moved in, moved to this house, she had asked me to go and um, and to do some ah, clean up the house. Ah, vacuum the rugs is what it was. Cause ah she wanted to put the furniture in, mop the floor. Ah, I went and got drunk. I came back. She asked me this at twelve o'clock, I came back in the house at nine-thirty. She had mopped the house and straightened the house up and her house looked good, and I jumped on her and beat her up....Because she, in my mind because she was trying to make me look like an ass. Because she could have waited on me to clean up, to do this. She asked me to do it....Now I just, I mean I just didn't only beat her up. I mean, I, I knocked out all the windows in the

> house with my fist. Ah I mean I'm standing here bleeding, my fingers, all these cuts and stuff like this on my hands. I'm standing there bleeding. Ah she's bleeding. I mean I, I've beaten her so bad and I, and I couldn't beat her no more. You know and I've beaten, I've knocked out all the windows. And just, I mean I just was a, a raging lunatic you know.

Scapegoating

Another man, a rapist, a child molester, and an alcoholic, said that he hurt women when he really wanted to hurt other men:

> I think the way that I felt about men is why I dealt with women the way I dealt with them. You know, because I didn't have the power over men but I had the power over women. I think women got the ass kicking, the ass kicking I wanted to give to men.

This is the man's idea of "ass kicking."

> I would snatch them up by the neck, you know, and apply just enough pressure to get them to consent, that they knew they were going to die. They would give in. I'd just tell them, you know, 'You're going to do every damn thing I tell you to do and you have no choice.'

This excerpt contains other themes, such as control and entitlement, and it illustrates the impossibility of reducing the phenomenology of violence to discrete categories. The themes and dimensions of violence are inextricably connected.

Proves You've Got Guts

The man convicted three times of attempted murder talked about how he handled another boy who had beaten him up the week before:

> I was about ten. And, ah, and sure enough the next ah Sunday this guy ah came to me again you know. And I guess I, I felt that he figured that I ran away once, once, he could make me run away again. And he had, he had more like his buddies and stuff with him you know. So ah I stood there and fought him. Ah, I beat him up, beat him pretty bad. So when I went home I was like a hero, you know. I got an extra helping of meat, an extra helping of potatoes. You know I, I really done something really great here, you know.

He was heartily reinforced for his violence. Meat has special meaning to him because he told with revulsion a story of how his aunt used to forage in the garbage of restaurants and come back home with "maggoty meat" for the family to eat.

Another man, a drug addict and physically violent recounted this story about his friends' reactions to his own injuries after being in a fight.

> I've woke up in the morning with this lip hanging out here, the side of my jaw this big [puts hand over left side of face] and my eyes swollen shut and my nose broke. And, huh, had my friends come over and we yucked it up about it. Hell of a fight, wasn't it? You know. Somehow I was a man then, you know.

Illustration Through an Individual Case Study

The following case illustration is of Mike (not his real name), who was in prison for kidnapping, rape, and attempted murder of a couple he picked up hitchhiking. His life story illustrates these themes and hopefully shows how interconnected these themes are.

Control

One man talked about how he used fear to ***control*** his girlfriend so she would not leave him. When she finally left him, he tried to commit suicide. Catastrophic fears of abandonment, however, appear to be part of his experience of violence, and using intimidation was an ***expedient*** way of keeping her in the relationship and perhaps temporarily assuring himself that he won't be abandoned.

> M: I think during that time I started to drink a lot, and I was getting more violent [14 second pause]. I think I really loved her but I felt that, ah, I felt I was driving her away from me. So, then I started using fear, put fear in her as a way to hang on to her.
> J: What, how would you use fear?
> M: Well, by attacking people in front of her. She would see me be violent, and I would tell her, you know, 'I don't think I could live without you.' You know, I would be real mean to her. Then, I'd make up with her, tell her how much I loved her, and, ah, that I'd probably die if I lost her. When we broke up, I did try to commit suicide.

Power

He provided an example of what he did to **control** his girlfriend: he used his raw physical **power** to hurt others. This story also shows how the notion of **vengeance** and perhaps restoring honor played a part in his violence. In being vengeful, I think he felt ***powerful*** and ***exhilarated***:

> One time I got into it with this guy, ah, that we followed to Dairy Queen and I beat him up. Then later on he brought some people back and four or five of them beat me up. So I traded cars during this time and I was driving by the recreation center one evening. And this guy was sitting in his car and he had his, he had slumped down in his seat and he was listening to music. So I drove out, turned around and came back. I had some quarts, quart bottles of beer so I drove up behind his car real quiet, got out, walked up beside his car and hit him in the face with a beer bottle. It busted, blood was squirting, and I went back and got in the car. I told him, I said, 'We're even now,' and I got back in the car and drove away, and she saw a lot of things similar to that happen, and she had to be terrified.

The terrible physical violence he perpetrated undoubtedly were experienced by Mike's girlfriend as terroristic threats. For him, they were something very different.

Protecting Self and Others

Mike not only was willing to use physical violence to terrorize his girlfriend and thus protect himself from losing her, but at 13 he attempted to murder his mother's boyfriend to avoid "breaking our home up. I didn't want to see my mom and dad split up." Thus, he was willing to murder in order to control his family situation. He also thought he would be ***protecting*** his father and himself from hurt. Getting rid of this man was, therefore, ***expedient***. He said

> My dad had an old twelve gauge shotgun...and it had a real long barrel on it. So, I got it, and I put a shell in it. I had a box of shells. I sat down beside the door, in front of the door. I was 13, I think. I knew what my mom and this guy was doing was really hurting my dad, and it was hurting me, and I had him to come in. I had the gun cocked, and I kept pulling the trigger, tried to shoot him, but the gun wouldn't go off...My dad had taken the fire pin out of the gun. That's why it didn't go off.

It is not clear whether he felt powerful and exhilarated as he sat waiting for his mother's boyfriend to open the door.

Commentary

I am going to depart from a phenomenological account and provide some background information that might place this man's experience of violence into a context. When Mike was about seven, he saw his father murder two black men. When his father called the sheriff, his father said the two men attacked him first. The sheriff accepted the story, although the father had a shotgun and the men he killed were not armed. Mike said he and his father found the two men trying to get into the father's truck. In his early teens, he witnessed a second murder. His uncle, older brother, and their friends beat a man to death with a shovel, stating the guy was a real loser and deserved to die. Somehow, Mike learned to excuse his father's unfaithfulness to his mother. His father used to go out with other women, including his mother's sisters. Mike had no comment about that, but his upset with his mother's infidelity was catastrophic. By the time he was eight, he hated his mother so much that he drowned the pet kittens that his mother would bottle feed. He said he was jealous of the attention she gave those kittens. When his mother started frantically to search for the kittens, he helped her look.

Expedience

Another aspect of his experience of violence was social: violence was a means of being accepted. When he and other boys hurt others, they would laugh at the pain they inflicted. Therefore, because being violent in a group earned him something, it was a form of **expedience.** It may also have been a form of showing you can dominate others, have **power** over them, and can **control** them. Perhaps it was a way of **proving that you've got guts.** He also learned that hurting others was fun, a form of **exhilaration**. He learned these lessons from his uncle and his older brother who used to let him tag along with them. He said:

> He [my uncle] was really violent [5 second]. Him and my brother, my brother used to drive around and they would hang out of the car, hitting people was a piece of rubber about this long. [He held his arms about 5 feet apart.] Then we would all laugh about it. I guess that's where I really first got into hurting people. I guess I thought other people really didn't matter, and I guess that's....I kind of got the message that the more violent you are, the more you're accepted.

Commentary

While very young, Mike was enveloped in cultures of violence. Violence became second nature to him. Not only did it make him feel *powerful*, help him *control* his girlfriend, restore his sense of honor through *vengeance*, but it was *expedient* in terms of gaining social acceptance and in terms of protecting himself and his father. He learned that other people don't count and that some are worthy victims, such as the black men his father killed and the man his brother, uncle, and their friends killed.

Entitlement

When Mike was about 16, he began raping women. In his accounts of his rapes of women, a sense of *entitlement* was strong. This is his description of how he got sex from women peers when he was a teenager:

> I think I didn't want to go through the trouble of, ah, building a relationship, having two or three dates and then have sex. I didn't want a relationship. I would talk to these girls. Back where I came from, people cruised around, and they have these little drive-ins where you stop at, and if you got a, ah, it depends on what kind of car you got. You know, I always had a sports car, and I could always pick these girls up, and I guess in my mind I was telling myself if they get in the car, it's okay to have sex with them.

In another conversation he elaborated on why he didn't want a relationship with women.

> I could have probably taken these girls out two or three times and had consenting sex with them, but I didn't want to put that much effort into a relationship, and I didn't really want to be around them anyway. I just wanted sex. (3 second pause) I guess my belief was that women would hurt you. You know, women would hurt me, and I didn't want anything to do with them, and then when I found out at about sixteen that they could make me feel good through sex that's all I wanted from them.

Not only might women hurt him, but Mike also saw girls who got into his car as tramps because they got into his car. This theme of deserving victim is part of the dimension ***entitlement*** and was common in the interviews. He distinguished between tramps and good girls. He said

> I think there were different types of girls, as far as I was concerned, because I had a, I had this one girl that I dated she was a Christian girl, a virgin, and I looked at her different than I did the girls that I picked up. I guess when I could talk girls into getting in my car I guess I felt that, ah, she's asking for it. She's a cheap little tramp so, ah, whatever happens to her she deserves it.

Mike believed he was entitled not only to rape women, but he saw the rapes as "practice" in "lasting longer," which, once accomplished, apparently was a factor in adding new aspects to his rape of his girlfriend. This was the same young woman he tried to scare into staying with him.

In the following dialogue, which is a continuation of the excerpt I just presented, he states not only did he want sex in the rapes but he wanted to humiliate the women. This dialogue continues to illustrate the themes of ***entitlement*** and perhaps ***gratification***.

> J: What do you think your goal was?
> M: To have sex. Maybe, now that I look back on it maybe it was some, cause them some humiliation.
> J: What did you tell yourself then?
> M: Sex.
> J: You wanted sex.
> M: Yeah.
> J: And there's a woman, and I'm going to have sex.
> M: Yeah. After a long time I would have premature ejaculation, but then the more practice I got the longer I could go.
> J: Uhuh.

M: That's when I went back to my girlfriend. Up to this time I would just, ah, force her to take her clothes off, and I would fondle her and then go home and masturbate, but then after I got some experience with these other girls...I would last longer then I started forcing my girlfriend to have sex.

His sense of ***entitlement*** to have sex with women included using them to learn how to have sexual intercourse. Once he learned sexual intercourse he moved from sexually molesting to genitally raping his girlfriend. His sureness about what he was doing gives further testimony to the idea that he had a sense of ***entitlement***.

His view of his rapes as "no big thing" for the women was another aspect of his sense of ***entitlement***. He defined the meanings of rape for his victims. He said

Well, the way I looked at it when I forced them to have sex, it really didn't hurt them. You know, they'll do this thousands of times between now and the time they're dead. So, it's no big thing.

In this statement, he is defining the women's reality for them, a form of interpersonal hegemony (McLeod & Gilgun, 1995).

Mike used his physical strength to enforce his sense of entitlement. Thus, his raw physical ***power*** expedited his rapes. He described how he used his entire body to subdue a woman:

M: I guess when I think when I started taking her blouse off she started resisting.
J: And how did you overpower her?
M: I was stronger than she was.
J: But what did you do?
M: I guess I just kept struggling with her. Probably wore her down. She,
J: With your arms? Or did you,
M: Yeah.
J: Use your legs and knees as well?

> M: Probably my legs too. I guess I used ever, how much force was needed. I never hit them during this time. I, I didn't have to. I was real strong.

Furthermore, he *enjoyed* forcing them to have sex, although he said he had some mixed feelings:

> M: I forced them to have sex I guess I kind of felt guilty about that, too, because I knew that I was doing something that she didn't want to do, and it also made me feel good too.
> J: What part of it made you feel good?
> M: (4 second pause) I don't know. Probably accomplishment. Maybe. I don't know, it's hard to explain.
> J: Yeah.
> M: That gratification.
> J: What kind?
> R: Well, I really liked the feeling of having sex.
> J: Okay. So it was, that was sex, sexual gratification. Any other kind? Or was that it?
> R: I think I felt relaxed after I had sex.

There were hints of several different themes of violence in this excerpt. The theme of humiliation might be here--as when he enjoyed forcing them to do what they didn't want to do. These behaviors are related to a sense of *control*. He also felt he accomplished something by overcoming their resistance. Therefore, there may be an element of a sense of *power*. Perhaps there was bit of payback in his experience of humiliating these women; that is, he believed that women would hurt him. Therefore, he would hurt them to restore his sense of honor, a form of *vengeance*.

Mike enjoyed the sex, as well. Thus, *exhilaration* and subjective gratification are also part of his experience of raping women. Since he did not elaborate on his feelings of guilt, I have to take his statement at face value while wondering if this is not a social desirability response, engendered by his therapy for his physical and sexual violence. Threaded throughout this account is the certainty of his sense of **_entitlement, power_**, and **_control_**.

Vengeance

Before he committed the crimes for which he was in prison, Mike felt locked into a marriage and a job he didn't want. He was as cruel as he could be to his wife, but she would not leave him. Though he had given up drinking, he resumed. These unhappy life circumstances sent him on the road in search of persons to hurt. He used his life circumstances to justify his crime. He told me that he used to blame the victims. If they hadn't been hitchhiking, he would not have picked them up. He said about the crimes for which he was convicted:

> I think I was looking for victims. I think I had a lot of rage built up, ah, financial problems. I was in a marriage I didn't want to be in. I don't think any, any of them's excuses, but I think it kind of contributed, to, ah, what happened. I think I decided to leave her. I tried for months to turn her so much against me that she would leave. Then I could blame it on her. She wouldn't leave. So on this day, I decided to go to D.C. [Washington, D.C.]. I went down and bought a camper for my truck.
>
> I went to my boss's house and borrowed some money from him, and I was laying all the groundwork, so I couldn't turn back. And I drove around Washington, D.C., for quite a while. I was drinking for the first time since my daughter had been born...and I guess when I didn't find a victim in Washington, I maybe gave up. Stated to go back home, and these kids were beside the road. So, I picked them up, and I think I knew when I picked them up what I was going to do. I think I was jealous because they were doing what I wanted to do, just be free and go where you want to go....I took them back in a subdivision that was being built, and I hit the guy in the head with the hammer. I didn't hit him real hard. You know, I could've killed him but, ah, [3 second pause] just hard enough to break the

skin, and I abducted the girl. I took her and raped her and beat her.

For Mike, hurting people somehow would restore him. When he found his victims, he was enraged because they were free and he wasn't. Somehow, taking his rage out on them would restore his sense of self. He was inflicting punishment on them for his own sense of self-injury. Thus, his acts can be considered acts of revenge.

Exhilaration

As with other acts of violence, there were other dimensions. For Mike, the acts of hurting, humiliating, and raping others was a tremendous subjective relief, and the sense of vengeance may have had a major part to play in this relief. He said

> I think the more I humiliated that girl the better I felt. The more pain that I caused her...I kind of felt like, ah, when Mount St. Helen's went off. You know, you can just imagine how that was feeling before it went off inside sort of. Maybe like a pounding headache, and then it exploded, but it must have felt like just a real relief.

Rape, humiliation of others--these are to Mike related to an incredible inner pressure and the acts of physical and psychological violence provide the relief.

In another interview, he described violence as relief in a second way:

> And particularly this last rape that I had. It's ah, it's really hard to explain the relief that I felt. It's kind of like all my burdens had been taken off, kind of like I'd been walking around with an elephant, and I finally dropped it. You know all my tension was gone, and I guess that's the way I released the tension then.

My Subjectivity

My subjectivity is continually engaged as I interview these informants. I intend to include my own subjectivity, but only insofar as this inclusion helps others understand my analysis. I want the focus to be on the informants and not on me. The following is an excerpt from something I wrote earlier (Gilgun, 1994) but which would give a flavor of a possible chapter on subjectivity. The following shows my responses to a rape-murder that Zeek (not his real name) committed and that I found horrifying. I was struggling with figuring out whether and how to be a connected knower, which is similar to Wax's idea of understanding as a precondition to research.

> I cried a lot the day after I talked to him--on Saturday, which was yesterday. I was glad to cry, and the crying no longer is about me and my losses. The crying was for that young woman and her family and the cruelty and irony and unfeelingness of Zeek, for the horror of waking up and seeing someone in your room, someone you'd recognize, and then have your life taken by his hands around your throat.

After thinking and feeling about this young woman's last moments of life, I appeared to have been able to connect to the perpetrator's experience of violence.
I wrote:

> I thought about writing a book, called *Evil Isn't What You Think It Is*. I'm learning about evil, the black, velvet of evil, the smooth softness of evil, like moving toward an orgasm, or even, like looking at a daisy in the sun, not knowing you are looking at evil.

This sense of evil arose not only from what he and other had said, but from how they described their acts; e.g., velvety tone of voice, hand and body movements, and how they looked at me. The last phrase about the daisy represents my thoughts about the young woman's point of view. She knew the perpetrator. She and the perpetrator lived in the same college dorm, and the perpetrator recounted an incident shortly before the murder of their accidentally bumping into each other in the college cafeteria. He said she looked right into his eyes, smiled, and said "Sorry." I wrote, "She was looking into the eyes of evil."

Understanding Competes with Rage

My growing understanding of evil appears to have competed with rage toward perpetrators and my inability to connect with them. I had violent fantasies which I, now, in my analytic framework, see as evil. At this moment, I believe, however, that there are degrees of evil.

> I have to say that I was furious and upset later thinking about this guy forcing himself sexually onto these women. I was sick at heart, too. I tried very hard to see it from his point of view, and I was not able to. I told a friend that I have had thoughts about asking someone for a gun and shooting him right in the forehead. I could not conjure up any milk of human kindness when I thought about him. What could have happened to him to make him think that this is what he could do to women?

A recent entry encompassed the multiple layers of meaning and emotion that compete for my attention during these interviews. An informant was talking about the death of his wife, whose murder had never been solved. When he began talking, I did not know his wife had been murdered.

> What got to me was not only this story, but how he told it. I felt somewhat foolish having been led by him as I was because it did not occur to me that his wife had been murdered. I was genuinely confused about how she had died until he told me about the lime pit. [Her skeleton was found in a lime pit. The man who found her knew it was a human skeleton because of the red polish on her fingernails.] It was disturbing to me to hear him talk about this because there was an erotic component from him, a heavy erotic component, a sense

of having gotten away with something and enjoying that, and a sense of being in a funeral home--a sort of heavy ominous, sense of finality. [I wonder if I was experiencing some of his grief?]

That's it. These are some of my processes as I attempted to understand subjective experiences of violence. I'm wondering--am I coming up with better understandings and genuine knowledge? I think I have a lot more feeling, experiencing, thinking, interviewing, reading, analyzing, and writing to do.

Humor

As this excerpt shows, learning about violence from perpetrators has been excruciating for me. I do not know if any of my potential audiences will want to subject themselves to such horrible stories. I thought of using many different ways of presenting the material so that readers can bear to read my book. I thought of using humor as well.

For example, one of my informants told me that he and his partner were burglarizing a woman's apartment when they heard the key turning in lock. His partner hid in one part of the apartment and my informant in the other. The partner did not realize that the top of his head showed. The woman saw his head and, apparently thinking it was her husband or son playing a trick on her, she tiptoed up to the burglar and said, "Boo." My informant said, "She scared Burt (not his real name) half to death. He jumped up straight in the air, and the woman said, 'Who are you?'" I have some funny stories like this. They may take the edge off some of the horror.

When I Don't Understand

Although my own experiences sometimes help me understand and interpret what my informants were saying to me, I often am baffled, as when hearing statements like the following: "When I hurt people, it gives me relief" or "I try to instill that fear in everybody's mind that's around me and say, hey, look, if you fuck with me, this is what's going to happen to you." I still don't understand how controlling people can be the high that my informants say it is. One man said, "I felt like God" when he told a woman to have sex with a dog if she wanted more crack cocaine.

Not only did she do what he asked, but he said the other people in the room thought it was hysterical. My God is not like this informant's, and I can't imagine feeling like God if I ever did something like that to another human being. I simply cannot connect with him when he told me that this was about control and power. I thought it was about outrageous horrible sleaze, of taking advantage of another person's chemical addiction. I certainly can't identify with the other persons who thought it was so funny. The informant even reported that these other people thought he was great because he got this woman to degrade herself to that extent.

References

Barthes, Roland (1978). *S/Z: An Essay* (Richard Miller, trans.). New York: Hill & Wang.

Brunswick, Mark (1994). Police think woman killed daughter, 2 1/2, and tried suicide. *Minneapolis Star Tribune*, January 11, 1B-2B.

deFiebre, Conrad (1994). Teen bravado played role in boy's death, complaints allege. *Minneapolis Star Tribune*, January 19, 1b, 2b.

Gilgun, Jane F. (2002). Social work and the assessment of the potential for violence. In Tan Ngoh Tiong & Imelda Dodds (Eds.), *Social work around the world II* (pp. 58-74). Berne, Switzerland: International Federation of Social Workers. (*invited, peer blind reviewed*)

Gilgun, Jane F. (1996). Human development and adversity in ecological perspective: Part II: Three Patterns. Family in Society. Presented as a brainstorming paper in the NCFR 1993 Preconference Workshop on Theory Construction and Research Methdology.

Gilgun, Jane F. (1995). We shared something special: The moral discourse of incest perpetrators. *Journal of Marriage and the Family, 57*, 265-281.

Gilgun, Jane F. (1995, November). "Voices in the Text: Identifying Them, Articulating Them," a paper that is part of a

Symposium I organized on Interpreting Qualitative Data, at the annual meeting, National Council on Family Relations, Portland, Oregon, November 15-18. Paper renamed for presentation: "Fingernails Painted Red: A Reflexive, Semiotic Analysis of a Case of Family Murder."

Gilgun, Jane F. (1994). Reflexivity emerges as central; What does it mean for understanding and knowledge? *Qualitative Family Research, 8 (2)*, 1-3.

McLeod, Laura & Jane F. Gilgun (1995, November). "Gendering Violence," a refereed poster session at the annual meeting, National Council on Family Relations, Portland, Oregon, November 15-18. with Laura McLeod.

McShea, Susanna Hofmann (1994). *Hometown heroes*. New York: Avon.

Myers, Amy (1989). *Murder at Plum's*. New York: Avon.

Scott, Kody "Monster" (1993). Monster: LA gang member tells how he started vicious life. *Minneapolis Star Tribune*, November 8, 1993, pp. 1E, 3E.

Scott, Kody (1993). *The autobiography of an L.A. gang member*. Grove/Atlantic.

Wax, Rosalie (1971). *Doing fieldwork*. Chicago: University of Chicago Press.

A Working Definition of Violence

Defining violence has been challenging. At this point, I have settled on three different definitions. I believe that at least one and sometimes all three fit any individual who perpetrates violent acts. These are my definitions.

> The term *violence* represents behaviors intended to gain submission, compliance, and power over others and that by-pass the consent of others and disregard the best interest of others; behaviors whose goals are the gratification and satisfaction of perpetrators and that by-pass the consent and best interests of others; behaviors intended to hurt others, either emotionally or physically.

5

Bobby and the Drug Store Robbery

In this article, Bobby tells his own stories in his own words. He shows that for some, violence simply is expedient. Perpetrators want something. They do whatever it takes to get what they want and don't think about what they are doing to other people. The even put their own lives on the line for what they want. It's hard to tell whether he enjoyed the robbery, the chase, and the fakery, but he did enjoy telling the story. Professionals who work in prisons call the enjoyment of telling tales of crime "euphoric recall."

The pharmacist didn't believe the robbery was true, like it wasn't for real for some reason. Then I hit him with the gun, and I put it in his side. Then I think he knew it was a real gun.

It wasn't a real gun. It was a pellet gun, a look-alike nine millimeter. It looked exactly like a real gun. You really couldn't tell. I hit him in the ribs. Then he knew it was for real. He goes, "Okay, okay, okay." I go, "Get on the floor. Get on the floor." So he got on the floor.

I usually just squat down, like to get behind the counters, but at that time I just didn't care. Things weren't going right. I wanted to hurry up and get out of there. That was my first thought--let's hurry this up. Just give me the drugs so I can get the hell out of here.

I saw this lady over by the cash register. There were people who started walking away. They were cashing their checks. They started walking away. I didn't even care about those people walking away. The lady in the front, she walked out the door.

I had one thing on my mind--getting those drugs. That was it. I just wanted those drugs. The lady was at the cash register [He snapped his fingers]--it was just an instant thing to say, "Give me all the money in the register" because I usually don't do that. I never touched the register at a drug store.

She grabbed the money. She came over and handed it to me. It was a big wad. I think it was like three thousand or something. I stuck it in my pocket. Then I told her to get on the ground. Then I concentrated on him. I forgot about her. She could've taken a gun and shot me or anything.

I was focusing on him. He came over with a little sack of drugs. It was really weird because nothing went like I was hoping it would go. I was pointing the gun at her while she was giving me money. He went and got the drugs. Now he could've went over there and got a gun and shot me.

I don't know if it was because I had so much alcohol in me or. I mean I just got done drinking about fifteen bucks worth of alcohol. So I don't know if that was it or it was like I didn't care at the time because I was in the mood then. The way I felt is I just didn't care. There was no sense of feeling bad, feeling any guilt, anything like that. I wasn't even really thinking about getting caught. I was just focused on getting the drugs. That was my total focus at that robbery. Then I caught the lady trying to crawl around the counter. I told her to get back.

There was no sense of that feeling of power and that feeling of control. There wasn't even that feeling. It was just, "Get this over with." I wanted those drugs, and I wanted to get out of there real quick.

Yet, I think after I got them and I started leaving, that's when the fear of getting caught really came in because the fear of getting caught, even, when I was doing that, was not even there. It was like I couldn't get this going fast enough. You know what I'm saying? That was my main thinking. I couldn't get it going fast enough. I couldn't get this over with. It just seemed like it was taking forever. It didn't last long at all. A couple minutes, tops. Three minutes, four minutes, tops.

When I was leaving, then, that's when the fear of getting caught came in. Boy, I didn't want to get caught. I just didn't want to get caught. As I was running away, getting away, then I felt this desperate need to get away. In other words, the fear of getting caught was there.

Then I committed another crime while I was doing that. I took, what do you call it? Hijacking. Car jacking. It was a van. It was a van that was parked. It was a Handy Electrician's van. It was really weird because I remember walking through Macy's department store next door to the drug store. I knew there was something going on. I was right. They knew. Macy's knew what was going on.

They knew that I'd just committed a robbery. I didn't know that at the time. I found out afterwards that lady who left the drug store, the lady at the front desk, she left right away. She went across the street, and she hit the button, the alarm button at the bank.

When she saw me heading for Macy's, she called from the bank to Macy's and said that there was a guy who had just robbed the drug store that was coming in their store. Well they must've notified security because I remember people looking at me. I knew something was up. I knew something was up.

I just had this feeling that these people knew in Macy's. How, I don't know but I just knew. I was thinking in my mind that they might have thought I stole something in Macy's. You know what I'm saying? That I was boosting or shoplifting.

Then when I went out the other side door, that's when I saw all the cop cars, vroom, vroom, shooting by. You know just tons of them all over. I remember seeing that van. I'm just thinking in my mind, I need a vehicle. I need a vehicle. None of this was planned. This was just a spur of the moment kind of thing.

I think a lot of time when I do crimes it is that way. It's the spur of the moment. It's just what's happening while the crime is being committed. You come up with different things or you get different emotions and feelings as it's going on. That's what I tell people a lot of times.

No robbery is alike. Every robbery is so different, so unpredictable. You don't know what's going to happen in them because you point a gun at someone—this one lady one time, she turns around and starts running down the aisle. It's like, Jesus, you can't shoot her in the back. You know, I mean,, but there goes your whole robbery. You try to hurry up, get the drugs. It's just, fucking crazy. Sometimes it's just crazy.

When I went up to that van, like I say, I guess there was a sense of power in that. I felt that surge of power. When I went there and opened that door and I said, "Get the fuck out of the van. Get out of there." I pointed the gun. Then that feeling of the power came on, whereas I didn't feel that at the drug store so much. The guy just got out of the van. He dropped the sandwich and got out. He just wanted out. Matter of fact, I told him to move over. I didn't tell him to get out of the van. I just told him to move over because I was going to hop in and take off with him in it.

He just dropped the sandwich, moved to the other side, opened the door and kept going out. [He laughed.] He kept going. Then the poor guy was using his cell phone. I think what was happening was they were on a call or something, and they got lost because he had a map and he had a sandwich.

He was looking at this map. The other guy was on the phone, "Where'd you say this place was?" This is what I'm assuming. Anyway, the other guy with the phone saw the guy jump out of the van. All of a sudden the van screeches away. So he starts chasing the van.

Then I heard his partner, "He's got a gun. He's got a gun." He's hollering at his partner to stay away from the van because I got a gun.

Well, by this time, I didn't even get out of the parking lot. The cops were right behind me. I mean I just seen those cherries. Then this sense of fear. My stomach just fell. God, I hate that feeling. It's like, It's over with. I got to go to jail. All this shit's going through your mind, but still that feeling of trying to get away is still there. I still attempted to get away.

That's what's so dangerous about that. I could've killed people in that high speed chase that ensued after that. There was one thing on my mind, and that was to get away, to go. They were right on me, about three, four cop cars with the sirens going. I had the truck going as fast as it could go, like sixty, seventy miles an hour down side streets, going right through stop signs. Just whoosh.

It wasn't even on my mind about getting in an accident or hurting somebody. It was just getting away. That was the only thing on my mind, was just to keep going, keep going, try to get away, try to get away. It was like this instinctive thing that I was doing. You know what I'm saying?

They chased me maybe a mile. I tried to make a turn. I couldn't. It was kind of rainy out. I tried to turn. I knew I couldn't make the turn so I tried to turn back, but the brakes were locked. So then I let up on the brakes, and what happened is just a corner of the van hit this car. I mean the whole van kind of went on its side. The van was on its side. I still did not stop. I still kept going. There was little bottles of these drugs laying all over. I could see they were lying all over so I started grabbing some of them up.

I kicked out the windshield of the van. I tried to crawl out the windshield. As I crawled out the windshield, I hit this car. I went up on the car, and I fell down on the hood. I seen my face was this far from this woman's face. She started screaming. A shoe came off. So I had one shoe on and one off. I got out on the street again. I tried to run. I fell down right in the middle of the street. That's when the officers they were surrounding me. They were circling me.

"I'm going to fucking blow your brains out. We're going to blow your brains out." All this. That's when I think I finally came to the [He laughed.] idea that I was caught. Even after rolling over, after the cops were all over me, I still felt this, this need to try to get away.

It's really weird when you're getting chased like that, what goes on, too, in your mind. There's a lot of things that was going on. The sense of getting away. There was even a sense of thrill there, too, with that. There was a thrill with all of that and excitement with all of that. Not at first but after the chase started getting to go, then it started getting exciting and thrilling and everything like that. I mean there was some excitement there. Tremendous feeling of a fear of getting caught. I think that added into the excitement.

Boy, it took a long time to really come to the realization that I was caught. In a lot of those police reports the police said that they came really close to shooting me. I remember a couple times they did because when I was pulling out of that parking lot with the van, there was an off-duty cop that heard all this stuff on his radio, and he tried to pull in front of me. When he pulled in front of me like that, I couldn't go anywhere. That's when the cops in the back of me jumped out of their vehicle and came around to the side.

I looked out the window just for an instant. I saw him point his gun. He was pointing right at me. I ducked down like this. He didn't want to shoot because that other cop was in front. Now if he hadn't been there I think he would've. He even stated in the report that he came real close to unloading on me, shooting me, because they saw me take the gun out and set it on the seat while I was driving. I had it stuck in my pants. It was uncomfortable. So I took it out, and I set it down so I could drive better.

Everything happened fast. It seemed like it happened real, real fast. At one point time was really slow—in the drug store, and then it was just "poof." All of a sudden it speeded up. Poof. It just goes. It just happened so quick, but the beginning, it seemed like it took forever.

I think as it progressed, though, and I think that happens a lot--with some—of my crimes. Things accelerate. Things start going. Then I start getting built up, more excited and stuff like that. When I do a crime I have the excitement and fear and whatever, but as they start to progress, by the time I'm done with it, man, I'm high. It's like "Whew. I even want to get high. Then I get the drugs and shoot them in my arm. You know what I'm saying? I get the loot, or the jewelry, or whatever it is. It's an adrenalin kind of thing. You just feel really hyped and really going. Real excited.

Wasn't too fucking exciting when they threw me in the back of the cop car, I'll tell you that. [He laughed.] It was over with. Coming down from that is just terrible. The realization of being there in jail. I was in the hospital. I even didn't give up then. I didn't give up then.

I mean I give up when I knew I was caught, but, you know what? I still was trying to figure another way out. That's when I started going. I was in the back, and I cut my head open. The cops were being pretty mean. They slammed the door on my leg and stuff like that.

I was in the back of the cop car. I knew that I was going to go to prison for a long time. So I started taking my spit and going [He moved his saliva around in his mouth.]. I was laying in the back of the cop car. I'm thinking, Well, how the fuck can I get out of this? I was thinking, Well, just pretend that you're really hurt, and they might bring you to the hospital. This was maybe five, ten minutes after they had me in a cop car. I was thinking about going to jail and prison. I'm kind of crying a little bit and feeling sorry and stuff like that. Then I start thinking, Well, try to prolong your going to jail.

The blood was running down my face. I was thinking, Well, fake like you're really hurt and maybe they'll bring you to the hospital." Maybe there's someway you can get out of there. So what I did is when the police started taking me down to the courthouse I faked a seizure in the back of the seat.

I start flopping a little bit, you know, boom, boom, boom, boom, boom. I fell off the seat. I'm on the floor, starting to flop. The cop looks back, "He's having a seizure. He's having a seizure. What should we do?" I can hear their conversation now. "What should we do? Bring him to the hospital?" This and that, this and that, this and that. What I did was I started doing with my spit. I was foaming it up, kind of getting it white. When I got to the hospital I stopped flopping and everything.

They put me in a wheelchair. The cops wheeled me in there. I was cuffed and stuff like that. They put me in an emergency room in the county hospital. They had me lying on this thing. The cops were right there. I couldn't get away. I'm thinking, Well, fuck. I'm in a hospital. Now how am I going to get away?

I'm thinking lying on this bed. There's blood all over my face. I'm lying on this cot and I'm thinking, Fuck. The nurse was looking at me. She was shining the lights. I'm thinking, "I better fake another seizure, and then maybe they'll keep me here longer. I was faking so I thought by them looking at me maybe they could tell that nothing really happened.

All of a sudden I started going spew, spew, spew. Then the spit that I was saving up like that started coming out of my mouth. It was white and foamy. "He's having another seizure, having a seizure." They're trying to hold my legs down. Then I quick stopped the flopping around.

I remember from the workhouse, this guy having a seizure. He told me that after he came out of the seizure, he says, "Boy, I'm tired. I'm just so tired." So that's what I told them. When you have a seizure I guess it drains all the energy from you. I think that kind of made them believe that maybe I really had a seizure because I told them, "I just want to go to sleep now. I'm tired. I'm tired." [He laughed.] I forgot all about that.

Then a doctor came in. They still didn't know my name. They kept asking my name. They put me in this holding cell in at the hospital. They got a holding cell down there. Put me in a holding cell. They kept coming in. They had me strapped down I remember. I just felt so bad. I knew I was going to prison. I was just crying. I mean just true hurt and sadness. I knew I was going. I was afraid heavy duty. I couldn't even see the tears were so welled up in my eyes.

I was thinking about my three sons and losing my wife Millie and my sons. . I can't even describe it. I just felt everything was all over. I was going to prison for a long, long, long, long time. I felt this tremendous sadness. One of the saddest times I've ever been in my life, I think, was right then, man.

This nurse looked at me. She tried to reassure me that everything was going to be all right. I start talking about my kids. I felt a real genuine caring come from that lady. I remember that. I really remember feeling that. She really cared about me. She felt bad for me.

Anyway, they shave my head. They just shaved a part of my head. I kept going, "Don't shave my fucking head. Fuck you. Don't shave it." He says, "I'm going to. Hold still." I said, "Man, I'm not going to let you. I'm going to sue you," all this because I didn't want to shave. They were just going to shave a big bald patch.

Well, anyway, they started asking these questions. They ended up keeping me overnight then. They ended up keeping me in the hospital. They took me upstairs. They had the lieutenant come in, a couple detectives. They asked for my name. I still wouldn't tell them my name. They get me upstairs. They got a cop on my door. They didn't handcuff me. Now I'm thinking, again, "Now how am I going to escape? How am I going to get out of here?" This and that. But I just didn't. They were just on me. There were two cops out there. They were young. They were on me. There's no way I could've gotten away, but I tried, you know. I tried everything I could.

I remember them wheeling me down to this room to take a CAT scan because I had convulsions. I had a head injury. They put your whole body in. Then the guy says, "You have to unhandcuff him." So he unhandcuffed me. This was a different guy. They were switching shifts. They had to pull two cops off the street to watch me. There were a lot of things going on. I kept looking at him. The door was here. I was over there. He was over here.

So there was a clear shot at the door, but he could've got there quicker than I could've. So I'm thinking of all these things, like, What am I going to do? I didn't have the balls. I didn't get the courage up enough to get up and run over there. Well, maybe there'll be another chance tonight, or whatever.

Then I went back to the holding cell. I got into my feeling sorry for myself, feeling real sad and stuff again. I was crying. Then another nurse came in—not the one I talked to before. She started asking about my kids. I started crying again. I felt this real tremendous sense of sadness. She says, "Have you ever been in trouble before?" I go, "Yeah." She goes, "So you know what you were doing. You made that choice." I just remember her saying that to me. I go, "Yeah, yeah, you're right."

That brought me out of that sadness. Then I started getting tough again. "Fuck you. Fuck everybody." I don't know why I did that. She was right. That's what it was. Screw everybody.

I knew I was going to prison for a long time this time. I figured maybe twenty years. It ended up being nine. But twenty years, I figured. It was just real overwhelming. I felt more sad because of the kids, I think. That's where a lot of my sadness was coming. This feeling inside me. Maybe I was feeling sorry for myself but I think there was a true feeling, feeling sad for kids, me losing the kids and the kids not having a dad. What Milly was going to think, and the trouble and stuff she was going to go through. That was there. It just was really sad.

Then they came the next morning and the county sheriffs shackled my feet. It was over with. I finally felt, yeah, they got me.

6

What Child Sexual Abuse Means to Abusers

This article shows that child sexual abuse is a form of violence. Perpetrators of child sexual abuses talk about the joys, pleasures, entitlements and revenge motives that are characteristic of other forms of violence. Some even believe the abuse is love and that children are equal partners. Some stress the importance of pleasing the children sexually.

Sexual abuse means many different things to different perpetrators, but the core of these meanings is emotional and sexual gratification. They describe sexual abuse as love, a thrill, a fix, play, a conquest, or revenge, but sexual and emotional gratification is what they want and get. Some say that the only time they feel good about themselves is when they have sex with children. Sexual abusers take what they want from children. They abuse their power over children and enjoy doing so.

In this article, perpetrators say in their own words why they abuse children sexually. These stories may be hard to handle, but they are the harsh realities that child survivors have experienced directly. To be emotionally available to survivors, we must learn to handle our responses to these stories. The stories also answer questions that many people have, such as Why do they do it? How can they do those things to babies? Who do you think you are?

Sexual Gratification

For abusers, child sexual abuse is an intense, highly erotic, highly gratifying sexual pleasure. David, in his early thirties, handsome, blond, and a business executive, sexually abused his toddler sons and daughters. He said about sexual contact with his two year-old daughter

I remember that high, and, boy, I wanted it. I wanted it. The high came after I ejaculated. That's the high I was after. I didn't get a high out of fondling her or that.

Beau, a construction company owner in his late thirties, said about the abuse of his thirteen year-old daughter and another unrelated thirteen year-old girl

To me, it's not the same as having an orgasm. I mean, it was thrilling, and it was exciting, but it wasn't what I was looking for. Bliss is the word that I would identify with that. There's a really satisfying feeling of everything is kind of relaxed. There doesn't seem to be any pressure. It's a real nice place to be.

Matt, in his early thirties, had sexually abused more than two hundred children, both children he knew and did not know. He said about fellatio by a child

It would feel like being on top of the world. Up until now there's no greater feeling that I can experience than having somebody perform oral sex on me. That is my ultimate feeling.

Henry, a man who exhibited his penis to young girls and women, beginning when he was about eight years old, said

I've been doing it for forty years. It's really got a groove in my mind. It's the highest excitement that I know.

He was "infatuated with all the excitement." His first victims were his sisters. "I practiced on my sisters at home," he said.

Angus said about sexually abusing his pre-teen teenage daughters

The attraction was the sexual feelings. It felt good. Good feelings. Pretty powerful. The good feelings were worth looking forward to.

Josh, 21 and pudgy-faced, said about his sexual abuse of children who ranged in age from six months to seven years old

> I'm worried about myself because a lot of people say I did it because I was abused, I did it because I was angry, and I wanted to take it out on them sexually. I did it because of this. I did it because of that. I don't understand that. I just felt like I just wanted to sexualize them. By sexualize I mean just get your rocks off or whatever in a different way, a sexual high.

Herb had intense sexual fantasies about boys between the ages of seven and twelve. He said

> I would masturbate to fantasies. I'd be looking at the boy's face, and he'll be smiling and stuff like that. I'll just focus on that moment. The more I look at his face, or the more I'm humping him or whatever, the excitement just goes up and up and up. When I decided to masturbate, it just make it that much more thrilling to me. When I ejaculate, it just makes it, to me, it makes it just feel twice as good.
>
> I'm with this individual and the individual with me. We are with each other. There was no denial in anything. Whatever I wanted to do, the other person was willing to do it. It just took me to some heights sometimes that I never believed that I can get that high.

Here are the words of George, a father who described what he did to his thirteen year-old daughter in some detail and the electrifying thrill that resulted.

> One night I was making my regular rounds through the house, making sure the kids were in bed, the doors were locked, the cat was in and stuff. I had gone down to my daughter's room. It was very dark. I leaned over to give her a kiss goodnight. When I went to brace myself on her bed, I actually touched her breast when I kissed her on her cheek.
>
> It was just like a shot of electricity through my body. I went upstairs and went to bed and tried to forget

about it, but it was just racing in my head. I didn't go back down in her room for several days after that. Eventually, I did go back down there and the same thing. Kiss her on the cheek, but this time when I touched her breast it was intentional. Then progressively it got to the point where I went down there, and I would touch her breasts over and under her pajamas while she slept, or I believed she slept. I would touch her with one hand, and I would masturbate with the other.

Seeking Mutual Enjoyment

Many perpetrators want the child victims to enjoy the sex as much as they do. For example, Tim, a social worker who abused children in his caseload, said of the prepubertal boys he abused

> I like things to be mutual in my relationships. I like to get what I give. I think that's true in my marriage. I think that's true with my victims. I did the same thing. I always expected them to give me what I gave them. I've read in books where some molesters think it's more important that they get their own gratification, and for others it's more important that they give the child gratification. For me I'd say it was equal, fifty-fifty. Without one or the other, I would have felt really crummy, really shitty about it.
> If I would have had orgasm and the kid didn't get any pleasure or vice versa, if I'd given it all to the kid, and he wouldn't return it to me, either way it would feel really bad for me. It was real important to establish a relationship with my victims where they would give as much to me as I would give to them. They would want as much from me as I would want from them. So it was all very sort of even or equal.

Tim seemed convinced that he was a nice guy. He could not admit to himself how absurd his words are. Mutuality is impossible when he has power over children.

Christian described the sexual abuse of his thirteen year-old stepson Seth as "a pleasing relationship, trying to please each other on both sides." Christian said that Seth told him, "I want to make you feel good, Dad." Christian said Seth also asked the stepfather to do the kinds of sexual touching that the boy enjoyed.

Dick felt bad when there was no mutual pleasure. He said about his stepdaughter Rosie whom he sexually abused for twelve years starting when she was four

> Sometimes I would feel guilty because I don't think that Rosie had an orgasm. I'd think it as if I were her husband.

Convinced of their kindness, these men would need a great deal of therapy and honest self-reflection to see the harm they have done.

Mood Enhancement

Some men describe sex with children as the pursuit of good feelings in order to enhance their moods. Dick saw sex with Rosie as a fix, that is, an activity that fixed how he was feeling. He said

> That's what I was thinking--I need a fix because I was feeling crappy. Maybe I didn't get the contract I bid for, or my wife and I had a fight about something where I'd rather go spend some time by myself but I can't. How can I tell my wife I wanted to spend time by myself?

Sexually abusing Rosie was a solution.

Beau used his thirteen year-old biological daughter Michelle in similar ways. He said

> For anything that bothered me, I knew that I could go to Michelle and get sexual gratification. That climax makes you feel really good. It was easy for me to offend against her like that, to go to her. I didn't really care from much about her feelings at that time. I just cared about getting myself satisfied.

Sometimes the sexual abuse is so gratifying that it temporarily transforms how perpetrators feel about themselves. Pete, a man in his early twenties who was a youth worker specialist in outdoor recreation, found that the only time he felt loveable and worthy was during sexual abuse. He said

> When I was being shown affection from a young male, wrestling, hugs, doing things together intimate, intimately, then I felt loveable. I felt worthy. I felt all of these things that I didn't feel the rest of my life, and the ultimate act of that is sex. There was sex. It was always leading to sex.
> Even if it never got there with every child with whom I interacted, it was always leading that way. The good feelings lasted, I want to say, probably a week or so. It probably would've gotten shorter and shorter had I continued on.

George said something similar about sexually abusing his daughter while he thought she was asleep. He was thirty-two, and she was twelve.

> The only time I really felt good was when I was acting out sexually. It was safe for me. It was like everything around me was so dark. I wasn't getting any good feelings from anywhere. I had convinced myself that I didn't deserve them. No one really knows me. They just know the image. They didn't love me. They loved the façade. I just felt miserable.

Comfort

These stories show how thrilling and comforting sexual abuse is for abusers. Some believed that the comfort was mutual, while others who thought of sexual abuse as a way of comforting children actually were actually comforting themselves. This is what Ben said

> I honestly believe that during the abuse that I was showing, that I was feeling sorry for Beth, because of the way Margaret [Beth's mother and his wife] used to nag

and bitch at her all the time, and it was like I was comforting her at the same time she was comforting me. That, oh, I was showing her a type of love.

He abused Beth for about four years, starting when she was seven or eight.

Infatuation

Some perpetrators describe feelings of infatuation with child victims. Tim said about the first time he laid eyes one of the boys he victimized

> I remember thinking, 'That's a kid I want to have sex with.' It's sort of like seeing a beautiful model. From then on I was, like, infatuated with that kid.... It was more of a feeling of excitement and arousal and infatuation.

He used the language of male-female courtship to talk about his experiences with boys.

> All of a sudden, you see someone across the room that you're attracted to, and then if you're able to somehow fulfill that fantasy, go meet the person. Ask her out for a date, she accepts, and you go.

Adam was so infatuated with a boy he molested for several years that he did not think of consequences. He said

> I felt so much in love with him that I didn't think that I was doing anything wrong, illegal or otherwise.

Love

Perpetrators often talked about love. David wanted his two year-old daughter to understand what he was doing was love. He said

> The feeling was, it's not a feeling—it's a thought. The thought was so doggone strong about making that connection with my daughter, that she understand that

> this is love....Wow. It was strong. I meant it with every fiber in my body. It was really important that she understand, and I make some connection from her to me, too.

Some described sexual abuse as falling in love. George experienced a powerful rush, a deep love, and a sense of how simple the relationship was compared to the complexities of his relationship with his wife. He said

> It was so powerful, so strong. It was such a rush. It was so powerful and so strong. It was such a rush because there was like that emotional element to it. It wasn't just a sexual thing. It was almost like my daughter was my girlfriend. It was almost like I was falling in love with her. It felt simple to love her.
>
> Our relationship was, it was comfortable, and it was easy. It wasn't all complicated. My relationship with my wife was so difficult and so complicated and arguments and the whole deal. My daughter just loved me. She just thought I was great, and she thought I was fantastic. It was very, it was just comfortable. It wasn't complicated.

The sexual abuse took place while his daughter was asleep or she pretended to be. Little wonder that the relationship was uncomplicated for him. He was unable to think about what the sexual contact meant to his daughter.

Christian, in his early fifties, described the sexual abuse of his thirteen year-old stepson, Seth, as a love affair.

> I didn't call it molesting. It was making love to my son....When I was having my relationship with my son it was like a love affair. It really was. It was real.

Beau, thirty-seven, viewed his relationship with his thirteen year-old daughter as that of a girlfriend and boyfriend, and stated, "It was almost like I was falling in love with her." He dressed her up in women's clothes and put make up on her when he took her to dinner in restaurants. Like many other perpetrators, he had a dream of marrying her when she was older.

> My ultimate fantasy with Michelle was when she got to be of age, which was twenty-one to me, that we would be married. It would be easy because our names would remain the same. We would have children together, and that they'd be beautiful children. They'd be all blond-headed, and they'd all have real deep blue eyes. We'd live happily ever after. I've never told anyone except my therapist and you. I loved her very, very much.

As a teenager, Chad said he was so in love with his younger sister that he wanted to marry her. He redefined the sexual abuse as mutual love.

> It wasn't really abuse. I didn't look at it as that way because it was both ways. It was like neither of us felt secure or, important, I guess, except to each other. I remember saying, 'Boy, if we weren't brother and sister, I'd marry you.'

Perpetrators who talked about love did not examine the contradictions in their behaviors. For example, perpetrators did not seem to realize that love is not love if coercion is involved. Children are coerced in many ways: through fear related to threats of harm, to physical size, and to compliance with authority. Love that is expressed through sexual behaviors does not involve one person being asleep or pretending to be, or one person having a wonderful time while the other is full of fear.

Mike's story shows some of these contradictions. Mike said he cared for his stepdaughter June so much that he dreamed about running away from her. At the same time, he admitted to scaring her into compliance by saying her mother would leave the family without her if she did not do what he said. He also thought he could turn her into a model and make money from selling pornographic photos of her. He said.

> I eventually think I would have run off with her. I thought about that. I would someday. That's where a lot of pornography and stuff comes in with people like child

> molesting and stuff, that they control, it controls their life so much that they finally get involved with child pornography and stuff like that, where they can manipulate the kids into doing things to make money for them. I think that was the road I was traveling.

Mike abused June for several years, beginning when she was about three.

Many other men who talked about incest and sexual abuse as love contradicted their avowals. Ben, for example, said, "What was between Beth and I was real, real special." Yet, he admitted that his daughter may have only wanted love and affection and not the sexual acts. Sometimes she did not want to go with him into his bed, but he picked her up and carried her there anyway. This is how Ben described what he did

> I'd go into Beth's room at night, you know, and I'd ask if she'd want to come in to watch TV in my room. Sometimes she'd say, 'Yes,' and she'd come. Sometimes she'd say, 'Well, I don't know.' I'd tickle her, and goof around with her a little bit, and then I'd pick her up and carry her into our room.

This man was as huge as a sumo wrestler. He looked like a walking haystack. Imagine how his nine year-old daughter saw him.

Christian, referred to earlier, was crushed when his stepson Seth testified against him in court. Beau used his daughter as way of attaining bliss, but at the same time, he dreamed of marrying her and having children with her. These men were clueless about what child sexual abuse means to children.

Sometimes perpetrators do not carry out their sexual desires. They spend a great deal of time thinking and planning and therefore commit a form of non-touch sexual abuse. Twenty-three year-old Marco, for example, wanted to rape his younger stepsister when he was between the ages of ages of thirteen and sixteen. He would peek in on her when she was in her bedroom or bathroom. Sometimes he watched her through her bedroom window. He said

> I masturbated and fantasized about me raping her and

> then giving her her first orgasm. She was going to love me and just adore me.

Marco did not understand that his stepsister was unlikely to love and adore him if he raped her, but he derived a great deal of sexual pleasure through masturbating to these fantasies. An unknown number of perpetrators peek in on family members and masturbate to sexual fantasies about them.

Not Incest but Love

For many father perpetrators, when other fathers had sex with their children that was incest, but what they were doing was something else. Christian said

> What I was doing was different. I was making love to my daughter, to my son.

Joe said

> We never had penile intercourse. I don't know why. I had it stuck in my brain that I couldn't have that. That was incest to me.

In addition, some abusers are outraged when they hear about other instances of child sexual abuse. Mike said

> I used to sit there and watch TV or I'd read something in the paper. I'd say, 'Look at this son of a bitch. He ought to get twenty years,' but I was doing the same thing. Mine wasn't that way. See, mine was love. There's a difference, you know.

Ben said

> The guy next door was an attorney. He abused his daughter. It came out in treatment that he abused another daughter in a previous marriage, too. I found it real disgusting.

Finally, some perpetrators have fragmented responses when they think about other men who commit incest. Dustin, a father incest perpetrator mentioned earlier, had at least three disconnected thoughts about a story about father incest that he watched on television. He said

> You feel disgusted. You feel disgusted at the men that are doing this on TV. At the same time you have a kind of a sexual thing going towards the girl that's getting raped. You're sexualizing it.

A few moments later, he said

> He's a piece of crap for raping his daughter. She's kind of cute. I wouldn't mind raping her, or making love to her. Never rape. It's always make love.

He did not connect the dots and see the contradictions. Instead, he jumped from thought to thought, image to image, with no connection between them.

Takers

There are exceptions to perpetrators' views of child sexual abuse as love. Some distance themselves from the children and depersonalize them. They take what they want, which is sexual pleasure and release, and have no sense that the children are human beings. Love and tenderness are not part of the experience for them. Marty said about his abuse of pre-teen Sophie

> When it was going on, she certainly wasn't a stepdaughter. I didn't have that at all. It was, oh, let me see, a thing. I could never look at her while she was doing it, not at her face. I could look at her breasts because when I was looking at those, that's something that turns me on. I can remember some times when she was masturbating me. Somehow I'd make eye contact with her, and I'd lose my erection.

Other men look for a quick sexual thrill that has nothing to do with love, as for example, Roland, who molested thousands of children in a twenty-five mile radius from his home beginning at about age eight. He continued until his mid-fifties when he was caught. He did not know the children and sought them in neighborhoods where no one knew him. He would go from one child to another, sometimes several a day, playing what he called "show and tell." He said

> It was just a powerful, I can't really describe it, like a drug addict or an alcoholic.

David, the man quoted earlier about how much he wanted the high, said about his three year-old sister whom he abused when he was a teenager and a star high school athlete and senior prom king

> She was just there as a, I don't want to say object. She was there to stimulate me and get me an erection so that I could masturbate.

Other men, too, state that the children are not children during the abuse, but as objects who satisfy them sexually.

Vengeance

When vengeance motivates sexual abusers, they want to hurt the children or someone else, sometimes family members who love the children. Juice, in his late twenties, sexually abused his partner Marguerite's seven year-old daughter Petal and enjoyed thinking how much he had hurt Marguerite and her family. He said

> I knew that Marguerite loved her kids with all her heart. I knew she loved her kids more than anything. I knew that right there would take the cake. It hurt her, the way that I thought it would. I wanted to. Like I said when I stepped into the house the day after I abused Petal and she had told her grandma. When I saw everybody crying I felt kind of good at that moment, seeing everybody falling out the way I thought they would, expected it to be.

Skip created an image of nine year-old Aria in his own mind and then acted on his image. He saw Aria as a "prick teaser," who "asked for it" and deserved to be raped. He said prick teasers "get you all worked up and they go jump someone else." Skip based his case on flimsy evidence. Aria was a "prick teaser" because when she bent over he could see her lace panties. He also overheard her telling other children that she "still had her cherry." Skip considered these actions an "invitation." His interpretations of Aria's behaviors meant one thing to Skip: This girl deserved to be raped. As he was about to rape her, she said, "You aren't going to take your cherry home." He enjoyed the rape. He said

> I shoved it in, tearing her vagina....I get the best ejaculation when I'm inflicting pain.

Marty was angry at his mother-in-law, whom he thought loved her granddaughter Sophie and Marty's stepdaughter better than any of the other grandchildren. He said about his mother-in-law

> There's been two women in my whole life who treated me this way [verbally abusive] and that I loved and wanted to love me but didn't. That was my mother and my mother-in-law....I got to the point where I would do anything to hurt her [mother-in-law]. I did.

He sexually abused Sophie. The first time he connected abusing Sophie with getting back at his mother-in-law was when Sophie asked Marty for permission to visit her grandmother. He said

> The first time it happened I was pissed off. I usually was when these things happened. I was mad at, at my mother-in-law. When I would get hot, and she wanted to go stay over there, my exact words were, when she said 'Can I go over there?' I said, 'Yeah, if you suck my dick.' That's what I said.

Skip and Marty, enjoyed the sexual contact, but they also enjoyed inflicting pain. This is sadistic, because sadism means just that—inflicting pain on others. Both men used common ideas about women as reasons for their behaviors. Many people believe that prick teasers deserve what they get. Ideas of revenge for perceived wrongs is wide-spread throughout the world, justifying rape, physical assault, murder, terrorism, and war. These men took these common ideas and applied them to children.

Play

Another pattern that characterizes how perpetrators thought about sexual abuse is sexual abuse as play. Joe, a father, in his mid-thirties, confused sexual behaviors with play. He said about the abuse of his eight year-old daughter:

> To me it was like slipping right back into childhood. I didn't masturbate until later, when she wasn't around.

It is doubtful that the daughter saw her father as an eight year-old.

Roland, who molested thousands of girls between four and six over a forty-year period, said about his abusive behaviors

> I thought that it was like a show and tell. I wasn't doing any harm. I figured the girls were young enough. They'll forget about it. The way some of them acted, like they didn't mind. They didn't care. I felt like I wasn't doing anything really wrong because I wasn't really physically hurting them.

Hugo, a man who acted out sexually since he was a young child, first molested a child when he was an adult. He said

> The first one was just more like seven year-old do: I'll show you mine, and you show me yours. Two kids were involved, and here one is thirty-one or thirty-two or thirty-four. She was seven.

He described the child not only as wanting the sexual contact and enjoying it but also as having control over when the contact would happen.

> I would fondle her. She acted like she enjoyed it. I says, 'Would you like to see my penis?' She said, 'Yes.' Actually

> I said, 'Would you like to see me?' She shook her head 'Yes.' I showed her my penis, erection. She reached out and grabbed it and stroked it.

As Hugo continued to talk, it became clear how complicated sexual abuse is. It can be hard to follow the logic of some perpetrators thoughts. Hugo said

> I figured she knew more about sex than I did—a seven year-old girl. After that we tried to get together once in a while. I tried to make contact with her but she had total control over the sexual sessions. If she didn't want to be fondled she told me, and that was it. She had control over me over that. I never pushed her any more than she didn't want.

In Hugo's description, the child changed from child to adult, to knowledgeable about sex, to being in charge. Throughout, Hugo thought of himself as a gentleman, never pushy, sometimes as a child with a child, sometimes as an adult who got together with another adult, and sometimes as an adult entranced by the sexual sophistication of a child. He also believed that she had all the power, and he was the child.

> It was like I brought myself down to her level, back down to a kid, because I did not feel like an adult, like I would with my wife. Do you love me? It was like I was a little kid talking.

Entitlement

Some perpetrators had a sense of ownership over the children that entitled them to do whatever they wanted. Mike said about is stepdaughter June

> She was a pretty girl--no question. I mean, other people say that, too. I looked at her at her other than just an object--also as a pretty girl. Then it would run in my head that she's not just a girl. She's mine and always will be. It would run in my head that she always will be mine.

Tim, the social worker mentioned earlier, felt entitled to sex with boys in his caseload, not because he was their father or stepfather, but because he had earned it. This is what he said.

> When I see children, people that are vulnerable and in need that I have concern and a desire to help and take care of this person, to give him what he needs materially or emotionally. That somehow either gets expressed sexually. It certainly arouses sexual feelings in me. Maybe it's that I feel that that's my payback for taking care of others, that I in turn get sex.

Damien, who worked in a public non-profit social service agency, said he got so much praise for his work that he began to feel he "deserved a little something" for himself. He felt "omnipotent," all powerful. He had sex with a teenage girl who was a client of the agency. He believed this was a "perk" for a job well-done.

Physical Violence

Some abusers physically abuse child victims, although most do not. When physical abuse occurs, abusers may want to beat and scare children into submission, punish them for not submitting, or heighten their sexual pleasure through inflicting physical pain. Herb, mentioned earlier, said, "I'll go to the extreme to do it." When his desires were not met, not only did he feel unloved and unwanted, but he typically went into a rage and beat and choked the boys. He described the beginning of an on-going abuse of a ten year-old boy:

> He was there by himself on his bike. I pulled him down by the back of his shirt. I didn't know whether or not he was going to holler, run or scream or whatever. So I punched him in the stomach. I told him what I wanted. He gave it to me. Ever since then it's more or less, I'm not going to... maybe it wasn't on a volunteer basis. It had a lot to do with the fact that maybe he was scared of me.

Herb, who was quoted earlier about how he "never believed he could get that high," went into murderous rages when the boys he was abusing in real time did not enjoy the sex as they did in his fantasies. He said

> I can see my hands around the victims' throats. I see those eyes bugging and the disbelief and the fear of knowing that they're going to die.

He described what appeared to be an out-of-body experience when he was about to kill children. He said

> As I was choking him, his face looked like David's, the person [a child] that I wanted so bad. This kid said to me, 'Herbie, why are you doing this? Don't choke me. Don't kill me.' That's when I came back to myself. I said, 'Damn, boy, what are you doing?'

> It's scary because it's like I'm totally outside myself. I'm totally somebody else. I can see myself doing this. When I come back and, and I catch myself, what I'm doing, and I say, 'Damn, what you doing?' It's like something has just completely took control of me and saying, 'I'm going to destroy this completely.'

Herb never said he had killed boys, but he may have.

Murder

Child abductions, rapes, and murders are sometimes outcomes of child sexual abuse. In such cases, perpetrators are beyond thinking about anything else but what they want. They are so caught up in their terrible acts that they are unable to think about anyone else but themselves and what they want. What they tell themselves about the abuse has far different meanings to others.

This is what a mother said after she discovered her eighteen month-old son dead in his crib.

> He literally beat him to death. I gave birth to that child. I carried that child inside me for nine months. I gave my

baby life. I did everything for that baby. Now he is gone. He had three skull fractures, a lacerated liver, a half pint of blood in his chest cavity, and a tear in his anus. I took my son into the hospital. They kept me on a suicide watch. After he passed away, my life took a severe downward spiral. Things have been getting better now.

The abuser was a "manny," a male nanny, trusted.

Discussion

Perpetrators have many different reasons for sexually abusing children: greatest feelings in the world, bliss, love, control, emotional and sexual gratification, and showing who's on top are just some of them. These various experiences have self-centeredness in common. It's all about them. They have callous disregard for the children and for others whom their behaviors hurt.

Child sexual abuse affects the entire family and creates fears in the hearts of parents. Of prime concern is the child or children who have been abused. However, parents, siblings, another family members may have deep and long-lasting reactions that include shock, disbelief, guilt, shame, and self-hatred. All family members require special care.

Wide-spread beliefs influence how survivors and those who love them respond to child sexual abuse. Many of these beliefs blame victims and mothers while protecting perpetrators. These beliefs make light of the abuse itself. As these stories show, perpetrators alone are responsible for child sexual abuse. What they want is all that counts.

7

What Child Sexual Abuse Means to Women and Girl Perpetrators

Women and girls also sexually abuse children, both boys and girls. Their experiences of abuse include affection, nurturance, and love. Like the men, they rarely think of the effects of the sexual acts on the children.

Women and girls who abuse children sexually report experiences that are similar to those of the men already quoted, but some give disorganized and confusing accounts of what the child sexual abuse means to them. These women had less therapy than the men quoted earlier. That could be one reason why their accounts tend to be unclear. They may feel guilt and shame. The men may feel less guilt and shame to begin with, they may have repressed their guilt and shame, and some may have worked through it.

Women who sexually abuse children are mothers, sisters, stepmothers, aunts, grandmothers, baby sitters, teachers, coaches, religious leaders and women who have other roles in children's lives.

It is important for professionals, parents, and policy makers to be familiar with the meanings of child sexual abuse to women and girl perpetrators. Survivors of abuse by women and girls often feel even more stigmatized because of wide spread-assumptions that only men abuse children. Girls sexually abused by women and other girls may feel especially strange about disclosing their abuse experiences. Boys abused by other boys or men may have fears of being gay. They also may feel unmasculine because they were unable to stop the abuse. Boys abused by girls or women may think they are supposed to feel as if have scored, but down deep they may feel stigmatized and shamed. Still others may believe that abuse by women is a form of love.

Nurturing, Mothering

Brenda, in her mid thirties, sexually abused a younger brother for three years when she was twelve to fifteen years old. She viewed her abuse as gentle and nurturing. She said

> He was five, six, seven when I sexually abused him--fondling, just touching, sleeping with, touching, sort of a nurturing thing.

She felt like a mother to him.

> I felt protective toward my younger brother. Momish. Kind of like a mom. I wanted to give them a better life, that kind of closeness.

It also appears she may have sexually abused other children in her family, as suggested by her statement that she wanted "to give *them* a better life."

She was emphatic that what she did with her brother was different from what her father had done to her.

> It wasn't like my father. It wasn't violent or threatening or scary and those kinds of bad things.

Like male incest perpetrators, she viewed the incest that her father committed as bad and scary, but what she did was nurturing.

Pleasure

Brenda also sexually abused toddler boys and girls in two different families where she was a nanny. She experienced that abuse as pleasure and as a release, but not as love and nurturing. She linked the pleasure she felt with children with the please and release she experienced when her father sexually abused her. She said

> He would like, when I was real, real young, he would put his penis in between my legs, and I would come. I mean I would feel pleasure. I would, you know,

and I don't know if it would be come back then. Do you know what I'm saying?

> I would have kind of a release from that. And so my masturbation was a lot like that. I was trying to give myself that same release. Which was also what I did with those young kids. Okay. I was try to give myself that same release.

Lorrie, in her mid-forties, sought pleasure with two toddlers she babysat. The abuse consisted of "their leg on mine." When asked if she thought doing this would be sexually stimulating or satisfying, she said

> You know, that's sort of what I thought I was going to do, and it wasn't. So it was like, okay, well, never mind.

She said she only did this once, and she thought the children were too young to remember it. Her account is a bit confusing. She found her sexual behaviors with children difficult to talk about.

Committed Love

Caron, in her early thirties, experienced passionate love for Tina, who was sixteen and a member of a church youth group that Caron, a youth minister, coordinated. Caron had been married for ten years and was prominent in the local arts community. She saw her sexual relationship with Tina was morally right. She said

> To become involved with Tina was more a moral, morally right to me, because I understood what was happening, and I felt right about it.

She talked about the sexual relationship in religious terms and compared her commitment to Tina to Jesus's commitment. She did not state what she thought Jesus was committed to, perhaps to his faith in God.

I didn't want to abandon her. I will take shit to kingdom come before I will bail out.... In some ways that is very, very strong to my religious point of view. It's very strong that you be there for people. It is very strong that that's the spiritual connection and understanding of who Jesus Christ was. He didn't bail out. He didn't go when he, and he didn't maybe have his self protection up either, when it really comes down to the story. And so religiously and morally, it, it, yeah, that's where I'm at.

Other survivors of clergy abuse, both boys and girls, state that the abusers used ideas from religion to explain what sexual abuse is. Often, clergy explain to children that what they are doing to the children is "God's love." Caron appeared to see her emotions toward Tina that way.

Women who believe themselves in love with children and teenagers have received a great deal of publicity in recent years. Women coaches and teachers comprise the largest group of women who state they are in love. The teachers and coaches often abuse boys, but some abuse girls as well. The women teachers and coaches typically are in their thirties and forties and the children are around 11 to 15 years old.

Male Coerced

Vonnie, in her early twenties, was in prison on a conviction of first degree criminal sexual conduct. She had held a teenage girl down while Vonnie's pimp raped the girl. She pled guilty to the crime. Vonnie said she took no sexual pleasure in participating in this rape and was afraid of what would happen to her if she didn't help her pimp. He had beaten her many times and felt completely dependent upon him.

Other researchers have interviewed women convicted of similar crimes and found their relationships with the men were violent, consisting of physical, emotional, and sexual abuse that was a continuation of childhood experiences. They described the women as willing to do just about anything the men asked out of fear of what would happen to them if they didn't. Vonnie fit that profile. She had been a street prostitute since the age of 16 and began running away from home to escape beatings and sexual abuse. Vonnie made no excuses for herself and wanted to go to nursing school when she left prison.

Muddled Meanings

Some women are unable to state how they experienced the sexual abuse they perpetrated. Lorrie, discussed earlier, provided a muddled account not only of the two children she abused in one family but also of a baby she abused in another family. She said of the very young child.

> The other child, I don't know what it was. It wasn't anything about the child. It was a very young child. It was a baby. Something about the house kind of creeped me out. People were weird. I don't even remember ever meeting the mother. I don't know. There was some, something funny about the family or, I don't know. I don't know if the guy reminded me of my dad, kind of a brash, really wealthy guy. I don't know. Those are the only things I can come up with. You know, I certainly can't tap into any conscious decisions that I made about that.

She was equally unclear about what her sexual abuse of the two toddlers meant to her.

> It's like once I did it and it was like, that was stupid or weird or didn't do what I wanted. I don't even know what I was thinking.

Incoherent Meanings, but Possible Comfort

Lorrie's account was unclear, but Pearl, who was in her late thirties, was close to incoherent. Not only it is difficult to make sense of what she said, but it appears that she did not understand that her behaviors with the children's behavior were inappropriate and constituted sexual abuse. She said she was naked in bed with her children in order to comfort them. The children ranged in age from fourteen to four. Enid was the oldest child and Phyllis was the youngest.

> You know, like, we went through a tornado three years ago, and so we were stuck in a hotel room. The kids were going swimming, and they came back and they were horsing around naked, because, there's only two showers at a time, and I was trying to find a place to live, and Enid kind of hit the roof, and I think Enid's reaction made an impression on Phyllis. More than anything they were doing, because I was right like, in the little. [She does not finish the sentence.]. I don't think too much could have been going on, but Phyllis talked about it at pre-school, so they had to report it.

[Question: The kids being naked, you mean?]

> Yeah, well, I think she more talked about how Enid—Enid thought it was really bad that we were naked and under the sheets together. You know, we had to talk about boundaries. It was certainly not something I condoned, but I didn't think it was—I mean we just lost—the tornado destroyed primarily the kids' floor. They just lost everything they had, and if they were going to find some self-comfort in their bodies, I was kind of ok with that.

Pearl appears to be saying that the older daughter Enid was very upset that the children and possibly Pearl were in bed together. Pearl justified the kids sexual touching by saying they needed comfort. She did not specifically say that she comforted them under the sheets not what they did to comfort themselves. Enid told teachers at pre-school, and they reported the incident.

Women who sexually abuse children often do not receive the intensive therapy that some male perpetrators do. This may account for the difficulties the women had giving clear statements about what the abuse meant to them. The men who provided the earlier accounts had been arrested, convicted, and ordered into long-term, intensive therapy. Therapy may have facilitated their abilities to talk directly about the meanings of the abuse, or they may not have experienced guilt or shame, or they may have experienced little or no guilt or shame.

The abuse that Lorrie and Brenda perpetrated never came to the attention of the law, while Caron experienced a police investigation but was not charged. Pearl had lost custody of her children, but child protection authorities did not require her to go to sex offender treatment. Vonnie was in prison while she gave her account, as the police charged her with criminal sexual conduct. She participated in a prison-based group treatment for women sexual offenders.

Summary

In summary, girls and women abuse both boys and girls. Their experiences of child sexual abuse may in some cases be similar to the experiences of male perpetrators, although a large percentage of women appear to have been brought into the abuse by a man who not only abused the children but the woman as well.

Recognition of abuse by women and girls is important for survivors of such abuse. The shame and stigma survivors might otherwise feel may further shame and silence them. Whatever experiences survivors have had must be widely recognized and understood so that survivors can feel safe to deal with the effects of the abuse.

Discussion

Few people realize what sexual abuse means to perpetrators. When they find out, they may be horrified. It's important to get beyond the horror and think about what survivors require to get through the effects of being abused. As we learn about the meanings of child sexual abuse, we see more clearly how unfair it is that child survivors feel stigmatized and ashamed of being sexually abused. Only perpetrators are responsible for acts of sexual abuse, as their own words show. Beliefs and attitudes about sex with children must shift to more accurate understandings.

Survivors know from experience what child sexual abuse means to perpetrators. Knowing what perpetrators say in their own words helps adults to become sensitive and responsive to child, teen, and adult survivors. The stories that perpetrators tell no longer can be unspeakable. Adults must be able to hear the stories that perpetrators tell so that they can empathize with survivors' experiences.

For survivors to overcome the effects of child sexual abuse, adults must be able to bear listening to their accounts. Adults also need to know appropriate, non-intrusive questions to ask. If they don't understand what survivors may have experienced, they cannot ask appropriate, helpful questions.

Anger, rage, disgust, and desire to punish are understandable responses to perpetrators' accounts, but adults must curb these impulses and be emotionally available to children. Sensitive responsiveness requires this.

In working with perpetrators, professionals must get beyond these strong negative emotions and commit themselves to understanding perpetrators. By doing this, professionals may be able to create settings where perpetrators can take honest looks at their behaviors and consequence of their behaviors, with no excuses and with a commitment to take responsibility for their behaviors.

Perpetrators may want help. Some want to stop because they know their behaviors hurt children and others. Many one-time adolescent perpetrators stop out of shame at what they have done, and this may be true for adults as well. Typically perpetrators—whether children, adolescents, and adults--may at first be unable to connect with the hurt they cause, but they may want to stop because they do not want to go to prison or to spend many years in prison.

As perpetrators grow in understanding, they may reach the point where they understand the gravity of their behaviors. Creating safety where perpetrators can confront the beliefs associated with sexually abusing children is a major task of treatment professionals, but perpetrators must be committed to change. Some perpetrators do not want to stop and do so only when they are put in prison.

Finally, rage, disgust, and desire to punish have led to social policies and programs that require hundreds of millions of dollars to enforce. In the meantime, survivors and their families do not have the services they require to work through the effects of child sexual abuse. Policy makers and the general public do not demand that survivors have services.

The meanings of child sexual abuse to perpetrators are difficult to hear, but important to grapple with. If we do so, adults will become more emotionally available to survivors and public policy will provide for public safety and for victim services.

Note: The story of Pearl is also present in *The: A Child & Family Assessment* by Jane F. Gilgun. Amazon, Kindle, Nook.

Further Reading

Gilgun, Jane F. (2010). The missing children in public discourse on child sexual abuse. http://www.amazon.com/s/ref=nb_sb_noss?url=search-alias%3Daps&field-keywords=Jane+Gilgun+missing+children&rh=i%3Aaps%2Ck%3AJane+Gilgun+missing+children&ajr=0

Matthews, Jane Kinder, Ruth Mathews, & Kathleen Speltz (1991). Female sexual offenders: A typology. In Michael Quinn Patton (Ed.), *Family sexual abuse: Frontline research and evaluation* (pp. 199-219). Thousand Oaks, CA: Sage.

Nelson, E. D. (1994). Females who sexually abuse children: A discussion of gender stereotypes and symbolic assailants. *Qualitative Sociology*, 17(1), 63-88.

8

The Thin Blue Line of Police Brutality

Sometimes we stereotype persons who commit violent acts. This article shows that people who swear to protect and serve can cross the line and be violent, in ways that are no different from disgraced convicted felons. In February 2009, a video camera mounted in a police car recorded several Minneapolis cops beating and kicking Derrick Jenkins who was handcuffed and on the ground. Later, one of the cops texted, "It was a good fight."

That quote sums up what most forms of violence mean to perpetrators. What made it a "good fight" is beyond me. Jenkins was handcuffed and on the ground. A half dozen cops were beating and kicking them. What makes that a good fight?

This violent act is no different from the thousands of other violent acts that I have listened to in the 25 years that I interviewed the men in prison for research on violence. Those prison inmates enjoyed violence while they vastly overpowered the people they victimized. A big man throwing his small wife through a picture window because she had talked to another man. Three men and a woman beating another man to death. These convicted felons told me they use violence as a high, to feel the rush, to redress a wrong, to earn or keep respect, to restore honor, and to be part of a group. A few thought murder and physical assault solved problems for them, or was just part of running a drug business. These cops sound no different from the young men who stalked and beat black men in Jackson, Mississippi, whose story I tell in Chapter 2 of this book.

Violent people believe victims deserve it. They decide who their victims are, and they act on their beliefs. A man beats a woman because women are supposed to respect men, and, according to him, she did not. A cop brutalizes a black man because according to him black men are dangerous. And they enjoy themselves.

At the time cops—and anyone else—commit violence, they are acting on deeply held beliefs. If they have rational moments, they know these beliefs are false stereotypes. The rush to violence is so powerful that cops—and anyone else—suspend their judgment and give in to the enjoyment of abusing their power over others. It's a rush, a badge of honor, fun. Their beliefs give them permission to indulge their violence. As one man said after a bar fight

> I've woken up in the morning with this lip hanging out here, eyes swollen shut, and my nose broken. I had my friends come over. We yucked it up. 'Ha, ha. That was a hell of a fight, wasn't it?' Somehow I was a man then.

Another man enjoyed instilling fear in others. He said

> My family's afraid. The people outside my family's afraid. Friends of my family's afraid. My sister's girlfriend, her and her husband came over to the house one night. Her husband, like we got into an argument. I jumped up, and I grabbed him, slammed him up against the wall. Here's my sister crying. Here's this guy's wife—she's crying. I'm like, what are these people crying about? They're giving me this high, this, this feeling of control or power.
>
> I got power now over these people. They're telling me, 'Oh don't hurt him. Don't hurt him.' My sister, she said, 'You don't know my brother. Control yourself. He might kill him.' I've got this power. I love that. I love people to dress me up.
>
> Another man shot one of his dealers because the dealer had not turned over the money he had made selling narcotics. 'It was just business. Besides, I can't let anyone punk me out. I'd lose all respect.'

To stop violence, we have to understand violence. Violence is enjoyable and gratifying and sometimes a way to take care of business. Beliefs about victims justify violent acts.

The cops who are violent may not be much different from most other people. Violence is rooted deep in our hearts and brains. When we feel wronged or disrespected, few people do not think violent thoughts. When we are in situations where we think we can get away with violence with no consequences to ourselves, who is not tempted to experience the deep satisfaction of making others pay, teaching them a lesson, punishing them for some wrong that we perceive?

Ordinary people have something in common with rapists, murderers, and child molesters—and brutal cops. We think violent thoughts and may do violent things when we think we can get away with them. We commit everyday acts of violence, such as blaming others for our mistakes.

I am not saying that everyday acts of violence have the devastating effects of rape, murder, child molestation, and police brutality. I am saying that our everyday acts often hurt other people and in the long run contribute to conditions that make egregious acts of violence possible. We human beings do not want to give up the comfort and satisfaction that comes from committing violence in our hearts.

Solzhenitsyn in *The Gulag Archipelago* recognized something similar when he wrote "… the line dividing good and evil cuts through the heart of every human being. And who is willing to destroy a part of his own heart?" Until we face up to the satisfaction we find in the violence we commit in our own hearts, we will not do what it takes to prevent violence that does deep and long-lasting harm to victims and those who love them.

Cops who commit brutal acts, convicted felons, and those who get away with violence are human beings. What we have in common with them is the violence in our own hearts and minds that permits violence to continue. Why stop? I enjoy it. Those are the words of a convicted violent felon. Those words fit a lot of us.

There is a thin blue line between police brutality and the brutality of convicted felons. There is another thin blue line between the rest of us and convicted felons.

Background

In February 2009, a Minneapolis cop stopped Derrick

Jenkins for speeding in a 30 mile per hour zone. The cop wrestled Jenkins to the ground and handcuffed him. Several other cops showed up. The beat and kicked Jenkins while he was on the ground. A video camera in the squad car recorded the incident. The cops' report stated that Jenkins had resisted arrest and that they had used necessary force to subdue him.

Jenkins lost his license and was charged with resisting arrest and assaulting a police officer. The video contradicted the report. Police supervisors reviewed the video and concluded that the cops had done nothing wrong, but they did recommend that all charges be dropped, which they were. Jenkins was shamed and humiliated and did not protest what the cops had done to him. He just wanted it all to go away.

When a cop arrested Harvard scholar Henry Louis Gates in his own home in July of 2009, Jenkins decided to speak out. The FBI is now investigating the Jenkins case. Jenkins is considering a lawsuit. Like Professor Gates, he wants to bring race-based matters out into the public forum for discussion. The video is widely available on the Internet.

9

When Cops are Criminals

When cops engage in criminal acts, they are no different from the perpetrators they are supposed to protect the public from. In this article, I show how "dirty" cops take what they want, dehumanize victims, dismiss the significance of what they do, and possibly refuse to deal with emotional states and ideologies of masculinity that undermine their own oaths to protect and serve.

Once in a while, cops are dirty, no different from the crooks they are supposed to protect the public from. A case in point is the conduct of several members of the Metro Gang Strike Force in Minneapolis, Minnesota, USA. The conduct of these cops was appalling. They stole seized property, such as jewelry, laptop computers, and televisions for their own use or gave them to relatives. They raided homes, arrested persons for whom they had no evidence of gang membership, and seized their property. A state commission investigated, and now the Strike Force is now under FBI investigation which began in 2009.

What happened? How can men who swore to serve and protect turn into criminals themselves? Among the possible responses is that most cops in the Strike Force were honest. They upheld the law and respected property rights. This suggests that there was something special about the cops who crossed the line.

With more than 25 years experience in interviewing convicted felons, I have a few ideas about what happened. The cops who were criminals had criminal tendencies before they were cops. This is no surprise because a lot of us have criminal tendencies. Many people commit petty crimes when they think they can get away with them. Many of us would dominate others if we met no resistance.

Access

That is the situation of these criminal cops. They could dominate people they said were gang members. They could confiscate the property of innocent as well as people later found to be guilty. They had access to goods they seized. Apparently, there was nobody to stop them. They may have stolen a few small items and got away with it. That emboldened them to steal more items. They did. So it went until they were caught and brought disgrace upon the Strike Force and the entire police department.

Contempt for Owners of Record

The thieving cops may have regarded the actual property owners with contempt, making the owners into persons who did not deserve to own such valued goods. They may have believed the owners got the goods through stealing them or that they bought the goods through drug money. Whatever the particulars, it is likely that the cops disrespected owners and owners' rights to the goods. Some of these beliefs clearly are racist.

Entitlement

The criminal cops may have believed they were entitled to compensation for the many sacrifices they made as cops. Cops don't get paid much. Their jobs can be dangerous. Being a cop is tough on family life. These cops may have feel angry, deprived, depressed, and anxious. They believed they deserved these goods and the owners of record did not.

No Punking Out

Being men and then cops, there is a code that says you do not admit weakness. Depression, anxiety, and even feelings of deprivation are signs of weakness for many people, women and men included. If they admitted they were hurting, they were punking out.

Strategies for Prevention

The thievery continued for years. Three strategies may have prevented these shameful behaviors and saved the police force from public shame and condemnation, which few cops actually deserve. The three strategies are supervision, holding each other accountable, and redefining manhood and punking out.

Supervision

Had someone who had power over the cops who stole had caught them in the act and had they been punished, that might have stopped the problem immediately. There would have had to have been support at the supervisory and rank and file levels for the punishment. What happened instead was a lack of supervision.

Accountability

The police in general need to hold each other accountable. Instead they have a "no squeal" code of conduct, similar to the "no snitch" codes in prisons. I believe non-criminal cops knew some of their colleagues were stealing, but they turned the other way. They didn't want to squeal. Some may have told the criminal cops to stop. When the stealing continued, they did nothing further. The no squeal code works most of the time, but when officers' conduct is reprehensible and also threatens the reputation of all cops, the no squeal code has to be suspended.

In short, cops should police other cops. For the sake of public trust and the oath they took to serve and protect, cops must break the code at times for the public good and for their own good. Cops must be educated to understand that any cop behaviors that threaten their mission must be held to account. Cops must hold each other accountable for behavior that threatens harm to the public and to cops themselves.

Manhood

Real men do not abuse their power over others. They do whatever it takes to contribute to the public good and to the welfare of friends and families. The police officers' oath places special responsibilities on them. It takes a real man to admit that his state of mind is threatening his capacities to live up to his own oath. This state of mind includes grappling with racist beliefs, which for many, are outside of their awareness. Cops, like all of us, need to figure out how to deal with racist beliefs.

Besides racist beliefs, cops must grapple with their own anger, depression, anxiety, and a sense of deprivation that leads to entitlement. These states of mind are not unusual in the general population and not unusual with cops. If cops do not deal with these states of mind, they may not be able to live up to their oaths. Out of anger, diminished capacities related to depression and anxiety, and entitlement, they do things they would not do if they were in good states of mind.

The stressful and sometimes traumatic nature of their jobs makes cops especially vulnerable to anger, depression, anxiety, and deprivation. Some cops have untreated post-traumatic stress disorder. Cops, however, have a code that they must not show vulnerability. If they do, they are punking out and subject to ridicule, humiliation, and self-contempt. The belief that punking out is disgraceful is short-sighted. Such short-sighted beliefs must be replaced with the belief that it takes a real man to admit vulnerability. Only by dealing courageously with vulnerability can men be strong.

Discussion

Criminal cops harm the public and other cops. They erode public trust in the very persons who are supposed to protect the public. Cops holding cops accountable is a simple and direct solution. This requires challenging the "no snitch" code in any situation where officers' conduct undermines the oath to protect and serve. Supervisors and rank and file must support this kind of accountability.

Cops must grapple with racist beliefs that many people hold, as well as with beliefs about anger, depression, anxiety, and deprivation. Such beliefs in times of stress and hopelessness guide otherwise good cops to act badly and to harm the general public, themselves, and the men and women with whom they serve.

10

The Bishop Has No Shame

This article shows that at least one priest who sexually abused children experiences sexual abuse in ways that are similar to other perpetrators.

Like other perpetrators, Roger Vangheluwe, former Roman Catholic Bishop of Bruges, Belgium, experienced child sexual abuse as "a certain kind of intimacy that took place." He elaborated on this statement on live French television a few days ago.

> I have often been involved with children, and I never felt the slightest attraction. It was a certain kind of intimacy that took place.
> I don't have the impression at all that I am a pedophile. It was really just a small relationship. I did not have the feeling that my nephew was against it—quite the contrary.
> How did it begin? As with all families, when they came to visit, the nephews slept with me. It began as a game with the boys. It was never a question of rape. There was never any physical violence used. He never saw me naked, and there was no penetration.

Mr. Vangheluwe hit almost every theme that I have identified in my research on perpetrators of child sexual abuse. (See the next chapter, What Child Sexual Abuse Means to Abusers.) According to perpetrators, sexual abuse is love and intimacy, not abuse. They say, I am not a pedophile. This is not a big deal. The child I victimized liked it as much as I did. I did not force the children. What we do is what every one else does—adults in families sleep in the same bed as children. There was no physical violence and no nudity.

Mr. Vangeheluwe did not say he experienced bliss, but he probably did. He sounds like other perpetrators who said bliss and "the greatest feelings in the world" were what they were after.

Like every other perpetrator whom I have interviewed, this man did not realize that evil feels good and that evil is not what many people think it is.

Mr. Vangeheluwe made his statement on Thursday, April 14, 2011, during the fifth week of Lent, a holy season in the Christian Church.

Faith and Child Sexual Abuse

Actions such as these do not cause me to lose my faith. On the contrary, this terrible event shows me once again how important it is to question our relationships with God to make sure we are not fooling ourselves. We must be skeptical of what we think is our relationship with God. If we are not, we can mistake evil for good.

I believe this man not only experienced evil as good but that he also experienced hubris, which is an unquestioning pride in the self. He did not question his relationship to God. In a certain sense, he married Satan, at least metaphorically, in his sexual behaviors with children. These children looked up to him and trusted him. Like other clergy, he may have told the children that what they were doing sexually was an expression of God's love. This man took advantage of children while believing he was living the word of God. Satan is clever.

The next chapter shows what child sexual abuse means to perpetrators. The bishop's beliefs are similar to those of other perpetrators.

Part 2: The Development of Violent Behaviors

11

Two Boys, Similar Backgrounds: One Goes To Prison and One Does Not: Why?

Many people wonder how two children from similar backgrounds can turn out so differently. This article shows how this may happen.

Picture two boys growing up in the same neighborhood. Both are 10, live in middle-class neighborhoods, are intelligent, and witnessed their fathers beating their mothers. Their fathers beat both of them. Both experienced sexual abuse. The person who sexually abused Rob was his father. The person who sexually abused Marty was an older kid in the neighborhood.

One will grow into responsible adulthood: optimistic, a loving husband and father, and a dependable employee. The other will become a prison inmate. What creates the difference in these two lives?

Rob: Trust in Others

Rob confided in a friend named Pete when his father beat him and when he had worries about school, friendships, and money. He learned from Pete's father how to fix electronic equipment. He tried to be like his friend's father. He liked school and enjoyed playing with other kids at school and in the neighborhood.

As Rob grew older, his circle of friends widened. He developed hopes and dreams for the future. He kept a diary where he recorded secret stuff about his troubles in his family, his feelings for girls, and how his day went. He got drunk at a party when he was 16 and didn't like the feeling of being out of control. After that he drank only occasionally and not too much.

Rob got married when he was in his early twenties. He used to spank his six month-old son through his diapers, and he intimidated his wife, but did not hit her. Whenever his wife was afraid, she left with their infant and went to her parents' home. When his wife suggested therapy, Rob declared he didn't need it. He thought he was behaving the way any normal man is supposed to.

One day, he was alone after his wife had left during one of Rob's tirades. He noticed a broken toy on the floor. He had broken it in his anger. He remembered that his own father used to have tirades and break his toys.

He realized that he had become like his father. He cried for a long time, and then he phoned his wife. "I'm ready for therapy. Please come home."

He did individual therapy, couples therapy, and then specialized therapy for being a survivor of child sexual abuse. He joined Parents Anonymous and became a national leader. Rob needed help with his beliefs about how to relate to his wife and son, and he needed to learn new behaviors.

Rob's story shows that children with capacities for emotional expressiveness and emotional honesty may have issues with aggression in adulthood, but they also are likely to get help for their aggression.

No child who has experienced childhood adversities is invulnerable, but they have a good chance of becoming resilient, as Rob did. Resilience is the capacity for coping with, adapting to, and overcoming adversities.

Marty: Broken Trust

Marty, at the age of eight, confided in a teacher that his father beat him. He also wanted to tell the teacher about the older boy in the neighborhood who sexually abused him, but he thought he would wait to see how the teacher handled the news of his physical abuse. The teacher called his father, who said he had never beaten Marty. When Marty got home from school, his father beat him for telling the teacher.

Marty never confided in anyone again. Instead, he tried to be tough, like men he saw in video games and on TV. They didn't feel hurt or helpless. They took what they wanted. They were in charge.

By the age of 10, Marty was stealing from stores and harassing other children, physically and sexually. He was doing poorly in school At 11, he joined a group who stole and sometimes attacked others, vandalized property, and used alcohol and drugs. Marty told himself he was having fun.

At 14, Marty was in a juvenile correctional center. Five years later, he was convicted and sentenced to 12 years in prison for criminal sexual conduct.

Similar Risks, Different Outcomes

As children, Rob and Marty were both at risk for committing violent acts. One had on-going relationships with people he trusted and in whom he confided personal, sensitive information. Doing so helped him feel better. Positive experiences and relationships were protective factors.

Marty had some protective factors, but a pile-up of risk factors overwhelmed them. His life might have been far different had there been early and effective responses to his report of physical abuse at home.

Resilience

Many people have risks for outcomes like Marty's, but most people with these risks turn out like Rob because they have many positive factors in their lives that they use to help them work through the effects of these risks.

Such people are resilient, meaning they have learned to cope with, adapt to, or overcome risks, because they use the positive things in their lives. Rob, for instance, trusted Pete and Pet's family. He gained a sense of self-worth through his close relationships with them.

He never sexually abused anyone, and at a party when he was a teen, he stopped another boy from raping a girl who had had too much to drink. "He might have put something in her drink," Rob said.

Other people are not resilient. In Marty's case, he made a decision early in life never to trust anyone else. He was far too young to understand the consequences of his decision.

When we look at the numbers of children who are hurt and afraid, what can each of us do to help these children build the trust required to begin to deal with the difficult events in their lives?

Bridge-Building

Only trained professionals can provide hurt children with the extensive help they require, but people can become bridges for hurt children, bridges that lead to safe and secure relationships with competent professionals who can help children deal with the harsh realities in their lives.

In the best of all worlds, the children's parents will walk with their children across that bridge to professional help. When parents cannot do this, then their children will have a tougher time, but they may be lucky as Rob was and find a network of people who will care about them and stick with them over the long term.

References

Gilgun, Jane F. (2006). Children and adolescents with problematic sexual behaviors: Lessons from research on resilience. In Robert Longo & Dave Prescott (Eds.), *Current perspectives on working with sexually aggressive youth and youth with sexual behavior problems* (pp. 383-394). Holyoke, MA: Neari Press.

Gilgun, Jane F., & Laura S. Abrams (2005). Gendered adaptations, resilience, and the perpetration of violence. In Michael Ungar (Ed.), *Handbook for working with children and youth: Pathways to resilience across cultures and context* (pp. 57-70). Toronto: University of Toronto Press.

Gilgun, Jane F. Christian Klein, & Kay Pranis. (2000). The significance of resources in models of risk, *Journal of Interpersonal Violence, 14,* 627-646.

Gilgun, Jane F., & Alankaar Sharma (2008). Child sexual abuse. In Jeffrey L. Edleson & Claire M. Renzetti (Eds.)

Encyclopedia of Interpersonal Violence (pp. 122-125). Thousand Oaks, CA: Sage.

Gilgun, Jane F., Susan Keskinen, Danette Jones Marti, & Kay Rice. (1999). Clinical applications of the CASPARS instruments: Boys who act out sexually. *Families in Society, 80,* 629-641.

12

Tony's Pathway to Juvenile Detention

Sometimes children develop violent behaviors while they're receiving social services. In this case, child protection was involved on and off for years wth Tony's family, but appeared to have done little or nothing to help Tony overcome his risks for violence.

Maria knocked on the door. The boy who answered was yelling at the top of his lungs, "Hey, you fucker, I'm going to rape you. I'm going to rape you." This child, Maria found out later, was six-year old Tony, the child his teacher had reported for possible physical abuse. The boy had bruises on his face. Maria, a child protection social worker, had gone to Tony's school to interview him about the bruises, but he was absent that day. She thought Tony might be at home.

Maria followed Tony to the basement. The boy immediately joined his older brother Davon in assaulting each other with mop handles, lead plumbing pipes, tacks, and kitchen knives. Their three-year old sister Bettina hid behind a couch. Their pregnant mother Kanisha sat on the couch with her hands in her lap.

Maria grabbed the mop handles and lead pipes and told the boys to sit down. That lasted about three minutes before the boys once again were punching each other and jabbing each other with an undiscovered tack and table knives they had hidden from her.

In the midst of this mayhem, Maria tried to interview Kanisha. When she saw Davon jam a tack in Tony's eye, she grabbed Davon. Kanisha took the tack. Maria laid Davon on the couch and rubbed his back. This seemed to calm him. However, when Maria stopped rubbing his back, Davon grabbed the tack and went for Maria's eye. When she stopped him, he yelled, "I want you to rub my back!" Maria told him to ask nicely the next time.

Davon jumped off the couch and punched Tony in the left eye which immediately began to swell. More of the same continued while Maria confiscated weapons and tried to talk to Kanisha.

Kanisha told Maria that none of the fathers of the children will help her. Tony had been suspended four or five times this school year, and he was only in the first grade. The last time it happened, she was at the doctor's for a prenatal check-up and unavailable by phone. The school called her mother. When Tony got to his grandmother's, she whooped him with an electric cord. That's how he got the bruises. The boys had also told their mother that their father's new girlfriend's kids try to hump them in the butt when they go over there, but Kanisha sends them as she needs the relief. She said that the children are out of control, as Maria could well observe.

Kanisha agreed to call Maria with the children's medical insurance numbers so that Maria could refer them for evaluations. Kanisha signed the application for social services and then the action really got hyped. Davon started pounding on Maria's legs. Tony and his brother Davon retrieved their mop handle and table knife respectively and started pummeling one another. Then the irrepressible Bettina attacked Maria with the pipe and a faucet that Maria had not noticed until then. Kanisha sat helpless in the chaos surrounding her. Maria again confiscated weapons, restrained children, and backed out of the house.

The following day, Maria called the grandmother who freely admitted to using the electric cord on her grandson. She said that she did it to keep him from abusing her dog. She further said that things are out of control in Kanisha's household and that her daughter has suffered from epilepsy since childhood. She believed that her daughter is retarded and cannot manage the care of the children.

The grandmother also said she did not approve of the man Kanisha keeps company with because he doesn't have a steady job. In addition, the grandmother had informed Kanisha she will not help with the children as long as she keeps seeing her present boyfriend.

Expelled for Sexual Harassment

A few days later, in interviews with Tony's teacher and school principal about Tony's bruises, Maria learned that Tony had been expelled for sexual harassment after he told a second grade girl repeatedly that he was going to rape her.

Maria wrote in a report that the home is a dangerous situation for the children and their mother. Kanishsa, she reported, is skinny and six months pregnant. The boys are big for their ages. She noted that "Even their two year old sister is becoming assaultive in the dog-eat-dog environment."

She continued, "The boys are grossly violent toward each other and any other poor soul who is within hitting distance of them. I feel that they all need to be evaluated for oppositional defiant disorder and attention deficit hyperactivity disorder. The long and short of it is that the boys present a danger to themselves and others. Their little sister is well on the way to becoming just like them. I also think that Kanisha herself is in danger of harm as she is so totally incapable of controlling them." Maria ended her report with, "Keep your eyes peeled for your own safety."

Eight Years Later

Eight years later, Tony was naked in his cell in a juvenile detention center, with only a non-destructible blanket to cover himself. For hours at a time, he screamed, "I'm going to kick your ass. I'd going to get you. You staff member, you're a bitch." He urinated in his cell, through the opening in the door where staff pass his food, in the hallway, and on another child when he was let out of his cell to take a shower. He broke a water pipe in his cell and caused a flood. Tony had assaulted other children in the center. He had threatened to kill himself and to stab and sexually assault other children and staff.

Given his behaviors, the supervisors at the detention center felt they had no other choice but to confine him and strip him of any clothing or objects that he could use to harm himself and others.

Police Arrest Kanisha

At around the time Tony was in lock-down, Kanisha was arrested on the street for hitting Davon on the face with her purse, leaving welts and bruises. The police handcuffed her in front of the children and brought her to jail. They placed the children in a shelter. Child protection filed a petition the court for custody of Kanisha's children.

In an interview a few days later, Kanisha pointed to her purse and said with pride, "This is the purse I hit Davon with." The child protection worked decided then and there that Kanisha would never have custody of her children again.

No Action

During the eight years between Maria's home visit and Kanisha's loss of custody of her children, child protection services investigated six reports of abuse and neglect. Kanisha was the subject of four investigations. Tony was the subject of one for breaking into a neighbor's house and setting it on fire. Child protection consistently offered services to Kanisha, and she consistently did not follow through. The children were on their own with a mother whom child protection considered a vulnerable adult who has serial relationships with a string of physically violent men.

Over the years, Tony had amassed a long record of terroristic threats, sexual harassment, and physical assaults not only with his fists but with objects such as chairs and wood-burning tools. These acts would have been charged as felonies had he been older. In the state where Tony lived, children can be charged with crimes at age ten but not before. Too young to be charged with crimes, he was old enough to be dangerous.

Many Police Calls to the Home

Besides the six reports to child protection for abuse and neglect, police records showed multiple interventions for physical assault of Kanisha by the various men in her life. These men had extensive criminal records for drug possession, drug dealing, aggravated and violent assaults, and petty theft. The father of one of the children was in prison for murder. When they worked for wages, they had low-paying jobs as roofers, rubbish haulers, and construction workers that usually ended when they walked off the job or were fired.

Little Apparent Concern

Neglect of children by the agencies meant to protect them apparently is not a priority for U.S. citizens, nor opinion makers like politicians, billionaires, and journalists. How child protection cares for children reflects how the U.S. public wants them to care for children. If the public cared about children, they would demand policies that actually protect children. Calls for "no more taxes" do not justify egregious harm to children. "No more taxes" do not justify putting family and community safety at risk when abused and neglect children turn violent.

Discussion

Few parents want to harm their children. Rather, they are preoccupied with their own troubles and do not realize the harm they are doing. Child protection has the task of figuring out how to help parents to deal with their troubles so that parents can take good care of their children. Child protection cannot do this alone. They require the backup of research that explores how to motivate parents, and researchers need funding to do the research. Funding comes from taxes.

Child protection workers need training. There should be a doubling of the number of child protection social workers in the US. Today, they have so many clients that there is a high risk of even more cases like Tony's. Child protection workers need to be paid better so that they stay in jobs. The turnover rates in child protection are shocking.

We live in a country where many brag about their family values. Where are their family values when children like Tony pay the price of their indifference? Where is our own self-interest? If we care for children like Tony, we not only do good, but we protect ourselves and save money in the long run.

Cases like Tony's are common. They are part of a pattern of neglect by systems that are supposed to protect children. If the American public knew how many children receive the "care" that this case illustrates, there would be research on best practices, on-going training of child protection staff, and an entire system that extends Constitutional protections to children. In the process of doing what is right, the American public will also be protecting itself from children like Tony. Such children might have been helped if anyone in power had cared and had the foresight to anticipate the unavoidable consequences of egregious neglect.

Sometimes public policy is a root of violence. With the backing of public opinion, sensible policy for the protection of children can become the seeds of change.

References

Gilgun, Jane F. (2010). *On being a shit: Unkind deeds and cover-ups in everyday life*. Amazon, Kindle, iBooks, & Nook

Lederman, Cindy S, Joy D. Osofsky, & Lynne Katz (2007). When the bough breaks the cradle will fall: Promoting the health and well-being of infants and toddlers in juvenile court. *Infant Mental Health Journal, 28(4)*, 440-448.

Rivera, Ray (2010). Despite signs, agency did not help girl who died. *New York Times*, October 6, A25.

Summers, Susan Janko, Kristin Funk, Liz Twombly, Misti Waddell, & Jane Squires (2007). The explication of a mentor model, videotaping, and reflective consultation in support of infant mental health. *Infant Mental Health Journal, 28(2)* 216-236.

Weatherston, Deborah J., Melissa Kaplan-Estrin, & Sheryl Goldberg (2007). Strengthening and recognizing knowledge, skills, and reflective practice: The Michigan Association for Infant Mental Health competency guidelines and endorsement process. *Infant Mental Health Journal, 30(6)*, 648-663.

Zilberstein, Karen & Eileen A. Messer (2007). Building a secure base: Treatment of a child with disorganized attachment. *Clinical Social Work Journal, 38*, 85-97.

13

Jacinta's Lament: Happy Father's Day, Dad

Jacinta is a beautiful, gifted young person with a great deal to give to the world. Instead, at 14, she wants to be pregnant by her baby daddy. She is on probation for running away. With her history of physical aggression and untreated, complex trauma, it is only a matter of time before she is locked up. In this article I tell Jacinta's story and ask how she became who she is today.

Jacinta wrote a poem to her father a few years ago. A beautiful, gifted young person, Jacinta's current goal is to get pregnant with her "baby daddy" and beat up other girls who taunt her that baby daddy messes around. She is 14. Beginning with Jacinta's lament, I then tell Jacinta's story. I also make suggestions about how we can be of help to Jacinta and other young people in similar situations. In the poem, the words, spelling, and punctuation are Jacinta's. I have changed all names and other identifying details.

Dad just don't let go

Dad why did you let go?
Crying and missing you
Why dad why?
Can't find you in the stormy weather.
Scared when your not there with me
It don't make sence to me anymore
Crying and looking for you.
I'm dirty and lost
I can't find you
Screaming and shouting in the stormy weather
In the forest can't find you.
I see light I ran to the light

I see you waiting there for me
You hugged me with dirt and mud on me
but you didn't care
The sun shined on me and the dirt went
away and my hair wasn't dirty and wet
no more.
Hugging me so tightly
Dad just don't let go

Teachers wrote in Jacinta's school record that she was in advanced classes for reading and writing and a star in basketball and track gym classes. She was graceful and slim. A teacher noted that Jacinta had frequent stomachaches and appeared depressed. She falls asleep in school.

The school nurse reported that when she phones Lily, Jacinta's mother, Lily yells, "Don't waste my time." Lily then hangs up and refuses to come to the school. Jacinta lies on the recliner in the nurse's office until she feels better. The nurse said that Jacinta has conflicts with peers and has no friends. She further noted that Jacinta is "sad and worried about her mother."

Principal Calls Police

When Jacinta was in second grade, the principal of her school called the police because Jacinta had stolen an unspecified "art object" from another student. When the principal confronted her, Jacinta tried to hide the object in the janitor's closet. She then was "defiant and disrespectful." She also had stolen a spiral notebook and pencils.

The school social worker phoned Jacinta's mother Lily who said, "I want my kid out of that school." The social worker reminded Lily that Jacinta "has other instances of misconduct at school." Lily hung up the phone. The principal suspended Jacinta for three days.

What Jacinta Told Police

Jacinta could not explain to the police why she stole from her classmates. She said that her mother drinks too much and leaves her alone over night to take care of a younger brother and sister.

Jacinta's Home Life

Police records showed several calls within two years to Jacinta's home for domestic abuse. Jacinta's father Henry beat Lily many times. Jacinta and her siblings hid in a closet or under their beds. There were no reports that Henry beat his children. Henry was in and out of jail for domestic assaults, drug violations, and weapons charges. Ordered into chemical dependency treatment several times as a condition of stayed sentencing, he failed each time and was sent to jail for probation violations. He worked in construction. He left the family permanently when Jacinta was nine years old.

When she was six, Jacinta told her mother Lily that her ten year-old boy cousin had forced her to "go down on him," meaning perform oral sex. Lily reported the boy to child protection. Jacinta had a forensic interview and a medical exam. The interviewer said the abuse probably happened. The district attorney refused to prosecute. Lily was outraged and vowed never to ask for help again. Jacinta did not receive counseling or other services for the sexual abuse, nor did her mother and father receive supportive counseling and information.

School records showed that Jacinta's older brother, Damien, 14, had "a record of disruptive behaviors on the bus," loud and aggressive behaviors at school, and charges of disorderly conduct. In one instance, he threw a crayon at another child and hit him in the eye. In another, he rammed the heads of two other boys together. A girl classmate reported that he had grabbed her breast and told her she had "nice titties."

Family income was through public welfare. Lily was exempt from time limits on welfare because she was a survivor of domestic assault. Jacinta told a teacher that there often was nothing to eat in the home.

Community Life

A few years ago, Lily was in the backyard of her home when her children ran in from the front of the house to report that a white woman had called the children "niggers." Lily ran to the front of the house and saw a middle-aged woman standing by a car. Lily yelled, "Why did you call my kids niggers?" The woman said she just got there. She hadn't said anything. Lily punched the woman several times in the head. Lily's friends who had been with her in the backyard watched. Neighbors also were outside.

The police arrived. Lily told the police that when her kids told her a neighbor had called them "niggers, "I got mad." The woman she attacked was not a neighbor, but a woman visiting a friend who lived in the neighborhood. The woman she punched told police that she has a heart condition and had been afraid that Lily's friends would also beat her. She had red marks on her face.

According to the police report, as the police questioned Lily, her friends began to yell "white racist motherfuckers" and "you don't listen to black people because you think we're all niggers." The report continued, "One female was walking back and forth saying 'It's on now, motherfucker. It's on.'"

The reporting officer wrote further, "I tried to address the group. I asked if anyone had seen the assault. No one would answer me so I repeated the question."

Finally, he got some of the story from neighbors. Lily's children walked past a car. One of the girls scratched the car with a stick. A neighbor saw her do it. That's when a neighbor called the children "niggers." The police report did not name Jacinta as the child who scratched the car, nor did the report name the children.

Psychiatric Diagnoses

In the second grade, Jacinta began what became a long-term pattern of "jumping other students." She became increasingly isolated. She maintained high grades in reading, but did not do as well as she could in other subjects. The school psychologist reported that Jacinta may have an oppositional defiant disorder. A few years later, Jacinta told the school nurse that she hears and sees things that no one else does. The nurse asked Lily to allow Jacinta to see a neuropsychologist. Lily agreed.

The neuropsychologist said Jacinta may be developing a schizoaffective disorder that is characterized by mood swings, hallucinations, and sometimes aggressive and withdrawn behaviors. Lily requested a second opinion. Several months later, another neuropsychologist reported that Jacinta is fine neurologically but has an adjustment disorder related to a long history of untreated trauma. He pointed to witnessing domestic abuse, being home alone at night with the care of younger siblings, and Jacinta's history of sexual abuse. He also said it is likely she has experienced other traumas that he was unable to identify.

With both parents often absent and psychologically unavailable, he said the need for intervention is urgent. He recommended intensive family therapy and individual therapy for Jacinta and Lily. Lily refused services. She said that she is not crazy nor is Jacinta. Jacinta will grow out of her troubles, she asserted.

Subsequent Services

At the age of seven, right after the stealing incident in school, Jacinta became a client in a program whose goal is to promote optimal child development and to keep children out of the juvenile justice system. This program, called EXCEL, provides case management services that build upon relationships of trust with children and their families. With trusting relationships, the case managers offer families many different kinds of services. Parents and children can accept or reject any or all services offered.

EXCEL fulfills its goals when parents do all they can on behalf of their children, when schools become safe for children, and when children and their families are willing to deal with issues that influence children to behave in ways creates hurt for them and others.

Jacinta has had the same case manager, Scotty, since she entered the program seven years ago. Today, Jacinta wants nothing to do with Scotty. Jacinta is angry because Scotty recently advised Lily to call the police when Jacinta left home and was out of touch for a few days. Jacinta was on the streets with "her girl," her best friend who had run away from home. As Jacinta said, "She's my girl. If she's out there, I'm out there."

The police brought Jacinta to court for running away. She was on probation. If she does not stay out of trouble with the law, she will go to a juvenile correctional facility. Jacinta blames Scotty for her precarious position.

Scotty helped Jacinta receive psychiatric care. The psychiatrist prescribed anti-anxiety medication. She also recommended family and individual therapy for Jacinta. The parents did not follow these recommendations. Lily supervised Jacinta's use of medication by checking to see if the pill bottle had fewer and fewer pills. They did. Lily thought Jacinta was taking them. When Jacinta went on the run, Lily found pills under her mattress. Jacinta had hidden pills there for months.

Over the years, Scotty wanted Jacinta involved in intensive services. These services required parental participation. Henry was in and out of the home, not available because of frequent stays in jail. Lily consistently refused. As a survivor of domestic violence, Lily would have benefited from services. As a result, she often was and is preoccupied with her own issues and is unable to be an authoritative parent and safe haven for Jacinta and her other children.

Scotty works with Jacinta and her family with Lily's permission. If Lily does not want services, she can fire Scotty. So far, she has not. She wants Scotty in the family's life in the hopes that she can fix Jacinta. Scotty has been unable to persuade Lily to participate in the range of services that the psychiatrist recommended. Scotty believes that Lily has had far too many bad experiences with social services professionals to trust other service providers and what they offer.

Because the EXCEL program is voluntary, Scotty has no power to get a court order to push Lily into seeking services. No professionals who have worked with Jacinta's family have been able to win trust to the extent that she participates in services.

Many children find their lives change for the better with EXCEL involvement. The shock of a referral to EXCEL is a wake-up call, where parents realize that they have to do a whole lot of things to help their children. This includes dealing with their own issues, such as unattended trauma. Parents realize they have been emotionally unavailable to their children and have not provided a safe haven for their children. When parents become receptive to a range of services and opportunities, children begin to do better in school, at home, and in the community.

For example, had Jacinta and her family used services offered, Jacinta would have become the honors student she could be, she could be on the way to college, and she could find fulfillment as a star athlete. She would want to postpone motherhood until she had a stable situation for herself and for any children she would give birth to.

At this time, Jacinta is on the edge of becoming a young mother and a high school dropout. She is one fight away from being put in a correctional facility for failure to abide by her probation order to refrain from physical aggression.

What's Going on for Jacinta?

Jacinta's story stands for the stories of uncounted hundreds of thousands of children in the United States today. She is a talented young person with the potential to have a happy life and to contribute to the quality of our common lives. Like many other children, her life is marked with hurt, confusion, and rage. Society not only loses the contributions of these young people, but others also suffer along with them because of the aggressive behaviors that many show.

Jacinta and young people in similar situations cause others to hurt in ways that are similar to how they hurt. Furthermore, for some people, like me, the hurt of others hurts me, even if their behaviors do not affect me personally. With so many children in Jacinta's situation, we are paying a high price for our inattention.

As Jacinta's case manager said, "We are as strong as our weakest link." He also said, "Strong children mean a strong society."

In this analysis to follow, I trace the influences on Jacinta's life. Individual responsibility is part of the picture. This viewpoint, however, does not take into account the well-grounded idea that how young people think is laid down in the brains' neural pathways from birth and even before birth. Experiences shaped how Jacinta thinks long before she had a choice.

The following are topics that help explain how we as a society have permitted young people like Jacinta to grow as they do. You may have another analysis. My description of her life may help you to see things I do not. I cover the topics of race, gender, education, services, social policy, and values.

Race

In some circles, Jacinta is a pickinini, a niglet, and a nigger. Now that she is past puberty, she is a "'ho" for some. Many other sexually charged words may fit her as well, again for some people. She knows that. So does every black child in the United States. Her father is a buck, a jungle bunny, an ape, a coon, and many other "things" in the minds of many. Some believe he has an extra large penis and is sexually dangerous, just like any other black man. He has known this from his earliest age. Jacinta has, too.

Many people see Jacinta's mother through a screen of words like "nigra," "mammy," "Aunt Sally," and banshee. Many also think of her as a welfare queen. She knows this. So does Jacinta.

These terms dehumanize Jacinta, her family, and other African Americans. Jacinta's experience of these terms became part of her self-concept. They are embedded in her brain circuits as inner working models of who she is, what others expect of her, and what she expects of the world. These inner working models guide her in how she thinks she is supposed to behave and what she is supposed to accomplish in her life.

Not only does Jacinta live with the knowledge that other people see her as less than human, other people are likely to act on what they see in her. We do not know the kinds of everyday racism she has experienced. She is of African-American descent. A disproportionate number of children in similar situations are also African American. This fact alone suggests that being African American is a factor to consider if we want to make things better for Jacinta and other children in similar situations.

The principal's call to the police may have been an example of racism in action. As stated earlier, the principal called the police when seven year-old Jacinta stole from classmates. There is no way of knowing if he would have done the same had

Jacinta been white. Children steal at that age. Few do not. Simple instructions about property rights can make a big difference.

Jacinta required special care. At seven, she had apparent depression and actual disruptive behaviors. Teachers may have been afraid of these behaviors because Jacinta is African American. Had Jacinta been white, it's worth wondering whether they would have taken Jacinta aside, helped her feel safe, and then asked her what is going on for her. Did any of the adults think she could be upset? Sad? Doing what she has seen many others do? Just being a kid who needed to learn about boundaries and personal property?

In the stealing incident, adults "confronted" Jacinta. No one mentioned that Jacinta became afraid when confronted, or whether she felt disrespected. No one appears to have asked whether confrontation helps children feel safe. Jacinta was probably already upset. To be confronted would make her feel worse. That she became hostile and disrespectful and tried to cover up are understandable. She may have responded differently had the adults been authoritative, being clear that they cared about Jacinta and that they wanted to help her feel safe enough to tell the truth. Jacinta did not trust them. Under the circumstances, who would?

The United States has a terrible history regarding race. Our founding fathers and those who came later abducted strong young people from Africa to work on farms for no pay. We treated them like sacks of wheat. We bought them. We sold them. We often decided who could reproduce with whom. We dehumanized them with names like "nigger," "niglet," "house nigger," "jigaboo," "boy," "buck," "chattel," "Sambo," "spook," "spade," "macaca," "pickininnies," "jungle bunny," "ape," "monkey," "Aunt Jemima," "Aunt Sally," "Uncle Tom," "oreo," "coon," "darky," "golliwog," "groid," and so many other terms.

Today, such terms rarely are public. When they do become public, the consequences can be severe. Senator George Allen of Virginia, once thought to be a viable candidate for president, lost his re-election bid for the U.S. Senate after he called a 20 year-old campaign worker a "macaca" during a campaign rally. His use of the word created wide-spread disapproval. The young man was of East Indian descent and was videotaping Allen's speech for Allen's opponent. Allen lost his Senate seat to Jim Webb. Yet, just a few weeks ago, Allen announced he was running for his old seat, saying he regretted using the term. While public sentiment is against the use of derogatory terms, they are wide-spread among some groups of people, including George Allen and people who share his worldview and values. Allen may win back his Senate seat with the help of others who think like him.

Words encapsulate beliefs about other people. These beliefs translate into policies, programs, every day practices, and inner working models of those who hold these beliefs and those who are the subject of these beliefs. The history of discrimination against African Americans in this country is well-documented. Unequal access to safe and affordable housing, to education, food, jobs, and respect is part of being African American, with some much more discriminated against than others. Slavery itself is an historical trauma, a legacy that continues to affect African Americans today. The effects of discrimination continue for Jacinta, her family, and the families of many other children.

Disproportionate numbers of African Americans are poor, like Jacinta's family. They also are more likely to be in prison, to be high school drop-outs, and to have chemical dependency and mental health issues. These facts are not attributable to something innately wrong with African Americans. Like Jacinta, their experiences have influenced how they think and what they think they deserve.

Jacinta's father Henry may have had a much different life had he been born to a family where race was not an issue. Had he been born into a well-functioning, financially secure family, Jacinta would have written a much different father's day poem. In a well-functioning family, Henry's parents would have stood by him, guided him, and provided the kinds of experiences that allowed him to reach his potential. That did not happen. Nor did it happen for Lily, Jacinta's mother and Jacinta's siblings. It has not happened for Jacinta, either.

A task of African American parents is to socialize their children to understand and to deal constructively with the racist terms and racist behaviors that they encounter daily. Through direct instruction and through their own behaviors, they hope their children can thrive despite the possibility that racism may hurt them. Almost all of them succeed. Their children do well in life.

Jacinta's family did not appear to socialize Jacinta to understand and deal constructively with racism, if Lily's response to her children's report that a neighbor had called them niggers is an indicator. Jacinta had been exposed repeated to the kinds of responses Lily's friends had to the incident. Their responses show the depth of race-based hurt and anger. The friends used charged language to the arrival of the police. The police may have feared physical aggression but there was none.

Jacinta witnessed and was the target of racism many times in her life. This one incident shows how complex racism can be.

Gender

Gender plays a role in beliefs related to race. The experiences that children have vary by whether they are girls or boys. Henry fits the stereotype of the aggressive African-American man. Lily fits stereotypes of the neglectful African-American welfare queen. That she is physically aggressive does not fit dominant gender stereotypes, but she does fit the image of woman as "bitch," "angry black woman, and "cat fighter."

Jacinta's history of physical aggression makes sense in terms of her parents' behaviors. Jacinta did not witness her parents discussing their differences in calm and reasonable ways. Although there is no known history of child physical abuse in Jacinta's family, she witnessed her father beating her mother many times. She also witnessed her mother beating at least one other woman. Her older brother had a long history of physical aggression. She saw these behaviors at such an early age that she believed that this is how she is supposed to handle conflict. Her parents and older brother may have told her she has to stand up for herself. If sometime disrespects her, she must act right away, not with words but with fists.

Today, Jacinta fits gender stereotypes related to young, poor African-American young woman. She calls her boyfriend her baby daddy, she wants to become pregnant, and she fights with other girls to keep her baby daddy. While she still "jumps" other girls, her case manager reported last week that she is far more adept with aggressive words. This fits with beliefs about gender, where women are thought to be more verbally able than men. Her capacities for verbal aggression also fit her well-documented intelligence.

Education

Educators in Jacinta's case may not have known how important it is for children to feel safe in school. If they did know this, they had no idea how to facilitate safety for Jacinta. School could have been a safe haven for her. Her home was not. Instead, educators confronted her, labeled her as hostile and defiant, and suspended her. It is worth wondering what might have happened had educators recognized that Jacinta not only has experienced long-term trauma, but she has learned to deal with her trauma through aggression.

The nature of trauma is such that memories of trauma are easily evoked. When some war veterans hear a car backfire, in their minds they are back on the battlefield. When Jacinta experiences reminders of her own traumas, it is as if she is experiencing them again. She deals with reminders of her trauma in the way her parents showed her—through aggression. Aggression is the first response to threat from her earliest years in her own family.

Educators at her school apparently knew nothing about how children deal with trauma. They mistook Jacinta's behaviors as indicators of hostility and of poor character. They did not know that Jacinta's behaviors are symptoms of untreated trauma. Jacinta and children like her require safety first and then instruction about how to deal with stress and conflict in prosocial ways. The confrontational responses of educators created additional problems that they solved by suspending Jacinta from school. In that way, she became more traumatized and less able to deal constructively with her automatic use of physical aggression. Their solutions made things worse.

Not only did educators not know how to deal with Jacinta, they also did not know how to get Jacinta's mother on board. It is worth wondering what might have happened if the school nurse, the principal, or anyone else from Jacinta's school had consistently recognized how stressed and overwhelmed Lily was. If they had realized that they must keep her and other children safe. It may have taken some effort to connect with Lily. There is no evidence that educators knew how to do this of that this is the most constructive route.

Services

Jacinta's school did not have the personnel to provide the services that Jacinta required to feel safe and to create trust with Lily. Other professionals had limited impact. Scotty, the EXCEL case manager, served in an advisory capacity. Jacinta and her mother Lily were free not to take up any suggestions that Scotty made.

Child protection social workers, who have the authority to make court referrals, could have used "friendly" persuasion to coax Lily into accepting services for herself, for Jacinta, and for her other children. Unfortunately, child protection social workers have many cases and are have administrative pressure to close cases. They therefore did not have the time nor the funding required to build a relationship of trust with Lily. Like educators, few of them have the skills to build relationships with mistrustful potential service users like Lily.

Even if Lily had accepted services, it is not clear that there were services that would have been helpful. It also is not clear that are service providers in sufficient numbers who are competent to work with clients like Lily and her family. Service providers themselves are first to point out how difficult it is to find competent services. Even when competent services could be available, funding may not be. People in need of services go without them.

Even when there is funding, service provision often requires coordination among several service providers. Parents and children may have professionals coming in and out of their home several times a week, often contradicting and undermining each other.

Jacinta's story would have been much different had service providers received the training and had the time to build relationships with mistrustful clients like Lily, had competent services been available, and had services providers been able to coordinate what they offered.

Jacinta require intensive services for her trauma. Lily had a history of trauma that required attention if she were to create safety for Jacinta in the home. Besides the domestic assaults and the effects of racism, Lily's traumas are unknown. Her physically assaultive behaviors suggest that she, like her daughter, also witnessed a great deal of physical aggression.

The traumas Jacinta experienced include years of witnessing her father assaulting her mother, frequent absences of her father from the family, permanent absences from the home, experiences of sexual abuse, home alone at night with younger siblings, and school suspensions. She many have experienced trauma related to racism. She probably had experienced other traumas that only she and possibly her family know.

Jacinta received no help for these traumas. She was on her own to cope. Anxiety, hypervigilance, anxiety, depression, and antisocial behaviors are typical responses to untreated trauma. Jacinta had all of these behaviors. How she copes depends upon how she has learned to cope. She learned to cope through observing how others around her cope.

Jacinta is responsible for her own choices. A quick think, however, shows how limited her range of choices are. Her behaviors are not only logical to her, but necessary if she is to maintain self-respect. She will chose prosocial and self-affirming behaviors when she sees the advantages of doing so and when she is surrounded by a supportive network of persons who behave in self-affirming and other affirming ways. Furthermore, these others must affirm her efforts to be self- and other-affirming, and she must experience these positive behaviors as good for herself and for others .

Public Policy

Public policy and everyday practices have created a perfect storm where children like Jacinta grow into young people who hurt others and themselves. Rather than becoming contributing members of society, these young people eventually burden society not only in terms of the harm they cause but also in terms of how much they strain county, state, and national budgets. Public policy in the United States not only is inhumane and short-sighted but it is also destructive.

Legislators do not see the importance of research, training of service providers, and increased availability of well-coordinated services. Not passing legislation that supports families and children like Jacinta's is short-sighted public policy that is inconsistent with democratic values, such as equal opportunity and justice for all. They also do not see the fiscal responsibility of these policies. Present policies are fiscally irresponsible.

Today, public policy is based on no more taxes and financing wars that cost billions of dollars a day. The values that underlie these policies are not care and social justice but self-righteous selfishness. As a result, money to foster social well-being is in short supply. School administrators are laying off teachers and not hiring. Social service agencies are cutting back or shutting down. Services that were to be permanent are now gone. For example, programs for children who are sexually aggressive are disappearing for lack of funding. They are at risk to grow into adolescent and adult sex offenders.

Tax cuts and refusal to raise taxes on the super-rich result in fewer services today and much higher expenses for services and prisons into the future. The human suffering involved is not part of the thinking of the no-more-taxes lobby. More taxes for the super rich do not hurt the rich. The super rich still will have far more money than almost all of the people in the world. How much money and power are enough?

Dehumanizing Others

It is to the advantage of the super rich that we dehumanize groups of people. The public does not stand up for those whom they perceive as unworthy. Those who experience themselves as unworthy do not demand the wages that allow them to live with dignity. Dehumanization creates a cheap labor force and therefore more money for those who control resources. Jacinta and people in similar situations become who they are because of this kind of thinking.

Some of the no-more-taxes people are secret racists, at least they try to keep it secret from the public at large. They are quite open about the race-based beliefs in groups who share their sense of superiority and entitlement. They do not want to share the fate of George Allen, as much as they know through experience that politicians like George Allen get them what they want when they contribute to political campaigns, buy them gifts, and finance junkets.

The idea that strong children build strong societies is not a factor in current social policy. It takes third place behind no more taxes and limited government. It is hard to know when short-sighted public policies will end. What is clear is that our policies are creating situations where more and more children like Jacinta will result.

Discussion

The private troubles that Jacinta has experienced since she was born are connected to public policies and beliefs. She is now 14. She does have to take responsibility for her own actions. Making other choices is to her advantage, to her future children's advantages, and to the advantage of society as well. She can't do this through magical wishing. There is no magic wand.

Jacinta would have made different choices had she been raised in a family where the parents were psychologically present and who treated each other and their children with sensitivity and gentle, responsiveness that is contingent each other's developmental capacities and readiness to interact. Had she and her parents grown up in supportive families and communities where they experienced respect and had access to resources that support their optimal development, then Jacinta would have many more choices available to her. Jacinta has a limited range of choices. She can only choose what she herself has experienced, just as her parents have a limited range of choices based on their own experiences

Jacinta today requires services based on solid research delivered by competent professionals. She needs to surround herself with self-affirming and other affirming persons who notice her gifts and affirm her in them. She needs to experience the affirming guidance of others so that she experiences the advantages of choosing other ways of maintaining her sense of integrity and self-worth.

Jacinta has not had services that help her see the advantages of other choices. If things go as they have, she will continue to make the choices that she has seen others make and that she has made in the past. The choices that she has make sense to her. They are what she knows.

That the bright and talented 14 year-old Jacinta now hopes to become pregnant with her baby daddy is an American tragedy.

References

Ex-Senator George Allen Again Voices Regret For '06 "Macaca'" Remark (2011). Fox News, June 3. http://www.myfoxdc.com/dpp/news/politics/ex-senator-george-allen-again-voices-regret-for-06-macaca-remark-060311

Gilgun, Jane F. (2010). *Children with serious conduct issues: A NEATS assessment.* http://www.amazon.com/Children-Serious-Conduct-Issues-ebook/dp/B0035LDNUK/ref=sr_1_2?ie=UTF8&qid=1348866939&sr=8-2&keywords=Jane+Gilgun+conduct

Gilgun, Jane F. (2010). *The NEATS: A child & family assessment.* Amazon, Kindle, iBooks, & Nook.

Green, Ross W., & J. Stuart Albion (2006). *Treating explosive kids: The collaborative problem-solving approach.* New York: Guilford.

Hill, R.B. (1998). Enhancing the resilience of African American families. *Journal of Human Behavior in the Social Environment, 1(2/3),* 49 - 61.

Isom, D. (2007) Performance, resistance, and caring: Racialized gender identity among African American boys. *The Urban Review, 39(4),* 405-423.

Kimmel, M. S. (2008). *The gendered society* (3rd ed.) New York: Oxford University.

Lieberman, Alicia F. (2004). Traumatic stress and quality of attachment: Reality and internalization in disorders of infant mental health. *Infant Mental Health Journal, 25(4),* 336-351.

Manning M.C., Cornelius, L.J., & Okundaye, J.N. (2004). Empowering African Americans through social work practice: Integrating an Afrocentric perspective, ego psychology, and spirituality. *Families in Society, 85(2)*, 225-231

Mellon, J. (2002). *Bullwhip days: The slave remember: An oral history.* New York: Grove/Atlantic.

Myrdal, G. (1944). *An American dilemma: The Negro problem and modern democracy.* New York: Harper.

Patterson, O. (1998). *Rituals of blood: Consequences of slavery in two American centuries.* New York: Basic.

Poulson-Bryant, S. (2005). *Hung: A meditation on the measure of black men in America.* New York: Doubleday.

Schiele, J.H. (1997). The contour and meaning of Afrocentric Social Work. *Journal of Black Studies, 27(6)*, 800-819.

Tierney, John (2011). For the executive with everything, a $230,000 dog to protect it. *New York Times*, June 11, 2011. http://www.nytimes.com/2011/06/12/us/12dogs.html

Van der Kolk, Bessel A. (2005). Developmental Trauma Disorder: A new, rational diagnosis for children with complex trauma histories. *Psychiatric Annals 35(5), 390-398.*

14

Pete's Pathway to Prosocial Behaviors

Pete was on his way to having serious problems with violence, but his father did what it took to do right by his son. With two years of intensive work, Pete was on his way to doing well at home, at school in the community. This article shows that unstable parenting, trauma, and neurological issues sometimes are part of the mix that leads to the development of violent behaviors.

Pete is a 10 year-old boy who has an eight-year history of serious behavior problems. His behaviors have been so potentially harmful to himself and others that he had been placed in a psychiatric hospital two times, once at age five and a second time at age eight. His parents, Patrice and Larry, had divorced when Pete was two. Patrice had sole custody, and Larry paid child support but rarely saw his son.

The behaviors that led to Pete's second hospitalization included several episodes of aggression in school and at home that included throwing chairs and desks at teachers and other students, throwing and breaking a computer, threatening his mother Patrice with a knife, fighting with other children, and grabbing the breasts and buttocks of three different girls. At times, he was silent and withdrawn, refusing to respond to other people. He swore, kicked, screamed, and threatened others when they tried to interact with him when he wanted to be left alone. He had been on medication for mood issues for three years, but the medication appeared not be helping.

During the second hospitalization, Pete's psychiatrist said he showed a disorganized attachment style that resulted from what appeared to be complex traumas that he experienced over several years. The psychiatrist noted that Patrice's behaviors had traumatized Pete and that she had been unable to provide the safety and security that Pete required to work through his traumas, and that she. Further, the psychiatrist said,

Pete's father Larry had failed to provide a secure base and by his absence had contributed to Pete's issues with unattended trauma. Both parents have to step up to the plate, he said.

After several sessions with Pete's parents, together and individually, the psychiatrist concluded that Larry was the more able parent and that Patrice was unable at that time to parent effectively. The psychiatrist appeared to have accepted Larry's explanation for his absence from Pete's life. Larry said he had stayed away because of a contentious relationship with Patrice and because of a cocaine addiction. When he stopped using cocaine and became active in Narcotics Anonymous, he stated that his own recovery consumed his time. He assured the psychiatrist that he wanted his son to live with him, and he was prepared to do whatever it took to do right by his son. He had been clean and sober for two years.

Larry Awarded Custody

Larry then petitioned the court for full custody of Pete. Based on the recommendation of Pete's psychiatrist, the judge awarded custody to Larry and ordered supervised visits between Pete and Patrice every other week for two hours at a child visitation center. A child visitation center is set up so that the custodial parent brings the children in one door and leaves the children under the supervision of a professional. The parent then exists through the same door. The non-custodial parent enters another door about ten minutes later. The parents do not see each other. The visitation room is child friendly, with toys, games, computers, and child-size furniture. One or more professionals supervise the visits from a respectful distance, writing notes on the interactions between parents and children.

Patrice vowed to appeal the court decision, but she did not. Patrice is inconsistent in showing up for her visits. At first, Pete would have tantrums, throw things, and be inconsolable when she did not appear. After several months of her inconsistent visiting, Pete became more accepting of not being able to count on her.

The two years Pete has lived with his father have been the most stable of his life. He has made progress is self-regulation and executive skills. He now pays attention in class, is respectful to other students and to teachers, and complies with school rules. He is mainstreamed in math, science, and gym, while previously all of his classes were in settings for children with emotional and behavioral issues. He has earned As and Bs in school. Earlier in his life, he received Cs, Ds, and Fs.

Patrice's Background

When Pete lived with his mother Patrice, she had periods when she appeared to be loving and sensitive. She also flew into rages, or withdrew and gave Pete the silent treatment. Rather than foster a healthy relationship between Pete and his father, Patrice made critical remarks and accusations of extreme cruelty, which Pete never witnessed, but he could neither refute nor confirm her reports. This left Pete confused about his father and stressed when his father stopped seeing him. Patrice complained that Larry did not pay child support, when in fact he did, according to court documents.

Patrice appears to have agoraphobia, which is an anxiety disorder characterized by fear of leaving familiar places, such as the home. She works at home as a website designer. She reported that she has had an eating disorder since her early teens, characterized by binge eating and then vomiting. This may be partially neurobiological in origin. While a student at a college of art and design, she stole money from dormitory classmates and was expelled. Given the instability of her moods, she may have a mild form of bipolar disorder, called cyclothymia, but she has not wanted to get a psychiatric diagnosis. She said her uncle sexually abused her when she was between the ages of five and ten, and she participated in a girls' group for sexual abuse. She believes the sexual abuse has had no effect on her and in fact has made her a stronger person.

Patrice had top grades while in college. She worked for a software company for three years and made a lot of money. She met Larry a year after she left college. They married a year later. Pete was born two years after their marriage. Patrice may have had post-partum depression because Larry reported that after Pete's birth, Patrice was never the same. She alternated between despondency and rage. She did not return to her job at the software company. She had earned enough money to have a large savings account.

Patrice worked sporadically in the software field after her divorce from Larry, but she quit or was fired several times for emotional outbursts. While employed most recently, she threatened to throw scissors at her boss who fired her on the spot.

Patrice was an excellent housekeeper. Her home was well-organized and spotless, and she kept Pete on a strict schedule of meals and bedtime. In this one area, she was predictable. Pete was meticulously clean, and she dressed him in the latest fashions. Both she and Pete took pride in their appearance.

Neither parent remarried, although Patrice has lived with several men since the divorce. Pete reported that these men often beat his mother and sometimes beat him. He saw his mother defend herself with a kitchen knife several times. Pete denied that any of the man sexually abused him, but his sexual harassment of other children suggests that he may have experienced sexual trauma.

Larry's Background

Larry has had a long-term relationship with a woman, but they do not live together. Larry said he wants to keep his life simple until Pete is older and shows long-term stability.

Larry had been a cocaine addict for many years. He managed to keep his job as a financial planner while using cocaine mostly on weekends. After a prostitute whom he had spent the weekend on a cocaine binge accused him of rape, he voluntarily entered a drug treatment program, which he successfully completed. He pled no contest to the rape charge and received probation, which he served. He no longer is on paper.

He has been active in Narcotics Anonymous since that time. Larry has a hobby farm in the suburbs, and besides raising alpacas for their fiber and riding his three horses, he enjoys golf, swimming, and travel.

Effects of Parents' Behaviors on Pete

Patrice's unpredictable behaviors, criticism of Larry, erratic lifestyle with men, and Larry's virtual abandonment appear to have had serious effects on Pete's development. In addition, he witnessed verbal and physical violence and may have been sexually abused. Pete, therefore, experienced complex trauma, with no secure attachments with which to work out the effects of the trauma.

In addition, Pete may have a neurological issues related to genetic predisposition to dysregulate, passed down possibly from his parents. His father's cocaine addiction could have resulted from difficulties in managing his own moods and emotions. His use of cocaine could have been a means of mood enhancement.

Patrice's bulimia, agoraphobia, and issues with self-regulation may be possibly genetic in origin but could also be related to the effects of child sexual abuse and other trauma that she has not disclosed. Therefore, it's not clear whether or not Pete's parents have neurological issues, but they could. Some of Pete's issues could also be related to his neurobiology. Pete has had many traumas in his life. If he hadn't he many still have had behavioral challenges, if some of his difficulties are related to neurology.

Larry Gets It

When Pete moved in with him, Larry had been sober for two years and stated that he was ready and eager to be a full-time father. He complied with the aftercare requirements involved with Pete's second hospitalization, but he did not believe that Pete's behaviors were challenging. "All he needs is love," Larry said. "I've got plenty of that for my boy."

Once aftercare was completed, Larry sought no more services. He asked the psychiatrist to take Pete off medication, which he did, although he recommended a slow tapering off. Larry said he did as the psychiatrist asked. Larry continued to participate in Narcotics Anonymous two times a week. Pete participated in the children's group.

A month after Pete moved in, Larry contacted the social worker at the psychiatric hospital, distraught with Pete's behaviors. He had gotten into fights in school and had run out of the classroom and hid several times. He continually argued with his father about bedtime, household chores, and helping around the farm. He struck his father with his hand one time. Larry realized that he and Pete required supportive services. The social worker set up an appointment with Pete's psychiatrist.

Larry consulted with the psychiatrist the next day. He said he still prefers that Pete not be medicated, but that he is now willing to get involved in services. The psychiatrist outlined a treatment plan, and the social worker helped Larry with follow-through.

The next week, Pete began weekly individual and group therapy at the local mental health center. Larry participated fully in the treatment. Father and son began family therapy at the center every other week. Larry also participated in a support group for parents of children with special needs. Larry exchanged respite care with two other families so that he could take time to travel for his job. Through these many services, Larry learned the importance of consistency, structure, and authoritative parenting. Pete did not go back on medication. He seemed to thrive when he knew what Larry expected of him.

Pete and Larry have been heavily involved in multiple services for almost two years. Gradually, Pete's aggressive outbursts and angry withdrawal episodes decreased to now being rare. When stressed, Pete engages in a variety of prosocial and appropriate responses that include talking things over with his father and therapists, practicing appropriate means of self-regulation in therapy sessions, and using physical exercises, especially farm chores, to help him reduce his stress levels.

Pete is doing well at the moment. For him to continue to thrive, he requires the safety and security that his father has provided for the past few years. If Larry starts using drugs again and becomes emotionally and physically unavailable, Pete is at risk to revert to his former behaviors. Both Larry and Pete require on-going support and understanding of others.

15

Phil's Pathway to Resilience
1999, minor revisions 2012

The article shows a pathway to resilience that Phil described. Not only did Phil cope with cruelty in prosocial ways, but he had the intelligence to succeed in school, the good judgment to marry a competent woman and respond to her reasonable demands, and the social skills to succeed at work. He also did not have a sense of entitlement, as he showed appreciation for how important his wife Sal has been in the positive pathways he chose, with her support and the challenges she put to him. This is an adaptation of excerpt from a published paper (Gilgun, 1999).

Much of what motivated Phil to succeed was a pushback against his father's emotional abuse. Not only did Phil show a strong positive sense of agency in how he responded to his father's cruelty, but he had many other qualities that were factors in his success in life despite adversities. Agency means a sense of will to do or to be something. This excerpt from interviews I did with Phil is an example of how he became afraid he was stupid. He described a time when he was 16 and worked on his car with his father.

> We were working on a car one time, which is kind of--it sticks out in my mind, because I was lying underneath my car and working on it, and my shoulder touched his shoulder, and it burned. I just hated it. I never touched him otherwise. We never shook hands, never did anything. It just burned. So anyway, he said, 'Give me an open-ended wrench.' I got a wrench. It wasn't an open-ended wrench. He says, 'You stupid son of a bitch.' He says, 'You fucking kids are so stupid.' He rolled out, and he went and got his own tool. So what I did is that I went and I got a Sears magazine, and I studied the tools, what was what, so I could--so he would never have to do that to me again.

Learning the names of all the tools is a positive coping strategy. This was a prosocial response to his father's cruelty. He could have yelled at his father and done something to get back at him. Instead, he educated himself about tools to keep his father from call him names.

Confidant Relationships

Phil's prosocial responses helped him to develop a sense of competence in knowing tools. He also established affirming relationships with others. He had a life-long best friend named Dave in whom he confided most of his feelings and experiences, and, when he was 16 and had his first girlfriend, he told her his life story, leaving out only the sexual abuse. As an adult, he talked frankly to his wife about his problems at work, and she appeared to have been an important factor in his career success. In short, Phil talked to others about personal, sensitive matters and found that helped.

As a teenager, Phil found an alternate father in Bob, Dave's father, who affirmed his sense of self-efficacy. He said of Bob

> I think he liked me because I was industrious. Dave and I would go to Dave's house and Bob would help us, and we'd get into conversations.

He was at their house everyday. Bob taught Phil how to repair electronic equipment, and by the time he was 16, Phil was running a small business and making good money repairing small appliances, radios, and televisions. As Phil was learning how to repair this equipment, he sometimes made mistakes, but Bob was kind to him. Phil in turn would help Bob when Bob needed an extra pair of hands: He said, "Bob was a model for me. I would watch him and help him. If I got into trouble, Bob would help me." In other conversations about Bob, it appeared that Phil consciously sought to be like him.

Into adulthood, he attended vocational school and college where he acquired knowledge and skills that that eventually led him to head a manufacturing concern. He attributed his hard work in school as attempting to prove to his father that he was not stupid. He said

> I suffered from severe low self-esteem for many years. I went to trade school, and I couldn't get into the class. I wanted to be an electrician, because my father used to be a tradesman, and I couldn't study in school. I was a wreck. I was just the bottom of all the grades. I got into the Technical Institute, and the guy said, 'You're nuts.' I took the entrance exam, and I didn't know any math. He says, 'You can't be an electrician. You don't know any math,' and it was just a knife in my heart. I thought I could finally prove myself to my dad, and I couldn't do it. So I took this other course, industrial hydraulics, pneumatics. I got in there, straight A's. I just got a job, went back to night school and did the electricity course, took the refrigeration and air conditioning course, took electronics courses. I'd get all this stuff. I kept trying to prove myself to my dad and prove that I was smart. Then I was sick of trade school, and I went to college. Anyway, things started clicking in my life, and I still suffered from this self--this issue that I'm stupid.

Phil sought tutoring in math from Dave, Bob's son and Phil's friend from childhood, who by then was in dental school. This shows that Phil sought help when he needed it and maintained relationships with Dave and his family over many years.

Determined to succeed in school and to show his father that he was not stupid, Phil displayed a strong sense of agency. He succeeded, and that success led to career success, a success. Though Phil had a single explanation for his school success, I believe there were other factors as well: he probably liked to learn, he may have set high standards for himself in terms of the kinds of jobs he wanted, and he probably formed some satisfying relationships with some of his teachers, as he had formed such a relationship with Bob.

A Competent Wife

His wife Sal helped him deal with work stress by listening. She also was a capable household manager, which he recognized, although he put himself down--typical of persons who feel defective:

> I was like a big baby. I couldn't take care of myself. She [wife Sal] took care of me completely, totally. She was like my mother, and if I was angry about work, she'd listen. She would wash the clothes, clean the house, handle the bills. I wouldn't have to worry about the money. That was her problem, not mine. I would go to work, take my paycheck, give it to my wife.

He was married while in school, and Sal's taking care of the household as effectively as she did undoubtedly gave Phil the time to devote to his studies.

Sal may have been instrumental in his decision to join AA and to enter therapy. She fought with him and refused to give in to Phil's self-defeating decisions. When one of their infants died, Phil at first refused to go to a grief group, which was what Sal wanted. He said, "I fought. I did fight. I didn't want to go to that thing." He went, however, because Sal "fought with me" and "convinced me to go." She said to him, "You owe this to me. You do owe this much to me."

Sal's fighting with him and his becoming convinced was based on his desire to keep his marriage and to avoid abandonment. He said

> I thought that if I was going to save my marriage, because I think, come to think of it, Sal had threatened to leave a couple times, if I didn't start taking care of it, holding up to my deals, she would leave. That triggered my abandonment, and that made me react, and my abandonment came from my mother [who] would get into a fight with my father and grab her suitcases and walk out the door. She'd tell us kids that we were bad, and that she was never coming back, and we were on our own.

Phil responded to his wife's demands that he go to the grief group, which in turn led to his joining Alcoholics Anonymous and then getting therapy for his sexual issues. His response was based on a desire to maintain his marriage and avoid abandonment. In addition, as shown earlier, he had a history of confiding in others, although he didn't connect his decisions to seek help with that history. Thus, thus with the urging of his wife, he saw the possibility that various forms of therapy could be helpful to him.

Overall, then, Phil can be thought of as displaying resilience. He overcame adversities, and he displayed many of the coping, problem-solving behaviors that have been noted in previous research and theory. His fortuitous marriage to a capable woman who was willing to struggle with him over pivotal issues and his responses to her shows the interactional nature of resilience processes. Sal was an asset, but if he had not responded to her, she would not have become part of his resilience processes.

Earlier in his life, he also showed a capacity to make effective use of the resources in his environment. Bob, his best friend's father, was a remarkable resource for him; in turn, Phil responded well to Bob, learned a great deal from him, and then was able to build a business while a teenager, a business that increased his confidence in his abilities and that could have been a factor in his adult vocational success.

Interlacing of Risk and Resilience

Phil's history also demonstrates that risks continue to be interlaced with resilience processes. He succeeded in school, but his need to prove something to his father was a possible risk condition that appeared to be undiminished once he proved that he could succeed in school. Another example of possible undiminished risks in resilience processes is his responses to his wife after she threatened to leave him. Is being motivated by fear of abandonment, even partially, a sign that risks are still present and not overcome?

A personal quality that may have been a factor in his ability to respond to the positive persons in his life was his emotional expressiveness. Throughout the telling of his story, he is clear about how he was feeling at any point in his life. As an adult, as the excerpts from his interview demonstrated, he was able to maintain what appeared to be an emotionally expressive marriage. Emerging in my overall research program is the idea that emotional expressiveness is an essential component of resilience processes. I touch upon this in Gilgun (1996a & b).

As is clear from Phil's story and from others that I have not reported here, a person's will, or sense of determination, appears to be pivotal in how risks and assets are used (from Gilgun, 1999).

References

Gilgun, Jane F. (1996). Human development and adversity in ecological perspective, Part 2: Three patterns. *Families in Society, 77,* 459-576.

Gilgun, Jane F. (1996). Human development and adversity in ecological perspective: Part 1: A conceptual framework. *Families in Society, 77,* 395-402.

Gilgun, Jane F. (1999). Mapping resilience as process among adults maltreated in childhood. In Hamilton I. McCubbin, Elizabeth A. Thompson, Anne I. Thompson, & Jo A. Futrell (Eds.), *The dynamics of resilient families.* (pp. 41-70). Thousand Oaks, CA: Sage.

16

Do Sexually Abused Children Become Abusers?

Most children and young people who are sexually abused or who experience other adversities do not become abusers themselves. They cope with, adapt to, and overcome adversities in prosocial ways. The three stories in this chapter show typical positive coping styles. While there are individual variations, the stories have much in common. They include having emotionally available parents or other adults over the long-term, being emotional expressive themselves, desire not to harm others, long-term friendships with pro-social peers and adults, the desire and resources to be like these pro-social persons, avoidance of relationships with anti-social peers, rejection of beliefs that they come first and can use others for their purposes, competencies in school, athletics or other activities, and a sense of a positive future. Persons who cope successfully with adversities are said to be resilient.

An important question is whether sexually abused children become sexual abusers. Most do not. This includes boy survivors of child sexual abuse as well as girls. Many persons assume that survivors of child sexual abuse, especially boys, will sooner or later end up as abusers. This is untrue. Being sexually abused is not by itself a risk to become an abuser. Being male can be considered a risk factor because most perpetrators of child sexual abuse are boys and men, but still most boy survivors do not go on to abuse others.

Persons who do not become abusers have protective factors in their lives that help them to cope with, adapt to, and overcome adversities. Child sexual abuse is an adversity. For many children, it is a trauma that may affect the quality of their lives into adulthood and old age if no one helps them to deal with it. Most people traumatized by child sexual abuse do not become sexual abusers of children themselves.

Protective Factors

There are many protective factors associated with not becoming perpetrators when boys and girls have been sexually abused. They include having emotionally available parents, being emotional expressive themselves, desire not to perpetrate child sexual abuse, positive relationships with parents, pro-social peers and adults, both the desire and resources to be emulate these pro-social persons, avoidance of relationships with anti-social peers, rejection of beliefs that they come first and can use others for their purposes, competencies in school, athletics or other activities, and a sense of a positive future. Persons who cope successfully with adversities are said to be resilient.

Studies show that most perpetrators of child sexual abuse were not sexually abused in childhood and, in fact, had parents who were "good enough," about as competent as most other parents. On the other hand, many were raised by parents who were not emotionally available and sometimes were abusive and neglectful. Such parents undermine the development of sensitive, responsiveness. Abusers do not have the emotional capacities or the conviction based upon beliefs to resist desires for sexual contact with children, although some can be quite emotionally sensitive in other situations.

"Me First" Beliefs

Abusers have a "me first" belief that allows them to use children sexually. They may tell themselves a variety of things about what the abuse means to the children, but they are self-centered and self-absorbed. Their behaviors show that they also believe they have a right to take what they want. At the time of the abuse, they think only of short-term gains for themselves and disregard, dismiss, and distort consequences for the children, children's families, and their own families.

Some may have some moral values that tell them that these behaviors are wrong. They therefore turn things around and tell themselves that children want and enjoy it, that this is love and not abuse, or, if they know they are hurting children, that the children deserve to be treated badly.

Stunted Emotional Development

In addition to these beliefs, stunted emotional development is a major risk. Stunted emotional development means individuals do not have the capacities to deal with their own emotions in sensitive, responsive ways, and they lack the capacities to be sensitive and responsive to children and often to other people in general.

Some may give the appearance of being emotionally expressive, sensitive, and responsive, but because they desire and actively seek sexual contact with children, they are out of touch with the meanings of their behaviors for the children, themselves, and their families and friends. At their core, they are as alienated from their deepest values and emotions. Often abusers are also callous and insensitive to other people besides child victims, most often their intimate partners. Marital rape and wife beating are common when husbands sexually abuse children.

Case Studies

Being sexually abused is a risk for becoming an abuser, but most survivors have enough protective factors that they do not. These persons can be thought of as the wounded well. Some survivors have a few risks and many protective factors, but abuse children once or twice as teenagers and then stop. These persons can be thought of as naïve experimenters. The following are case studies of adult survivors. They had several risks for poor outcomes, but each had the essential protective factors: emotionally expressiveness and lack of interest in sexually abusing children. Two did not abuse children sexually, and one abused two children one time when she was in her early teens.

Wounded Well

Rob and Margaret were sexually abused in childhood. Rob's abuser was his father, who abused him while they went on camping trips in the summer when Rob was between the ages of eight and thirteen. The abuse consisted of Rob's father masturbating him and showing him pictures from *Playboy* magazine. Rob hated these episodes and came to hate his father who beat him and made fun of him as gay because he did not get erections when looking at *Playboy* while his father masturbated him until his penis was sore.

Margaret was abused in toddlerhood by her father a few times and by two other men one time each. Both men were family acquaintances. She hardly remembers her father's sexual abuse, but can recall the smell of beer on his breath, his sense of urgency and fear, his breathing, and the pressure of his penis against her vagina. The second time she was abused, she was about six and the abuse involved a man who lived across the street from her putting her hand on his erect penis through his pants pocket and rolling her hand around his penis. She was afraid to tell anyone. The man moved soon afterward. A few years later, she overheard her father telling her mother that the man had died. She was relieved and glad.

The third time, she was about twelve, when another man fondled her breasts. She was too ashamed and embarrassed to tell him to stop or to tell anyone what he had done. She simply avoided him, as she had avoided the man who put her hand on his penis. She did not tell about these abusive episodes because she was confused and embarrassed. She did not think she would be punished.

Emotionally Abusive Fathers

The fathers of both Rob and Margaret were alcoholics and were emotionally abusive. Neither of their mothers did much to stop the emotional abuse and were sometimes neglectful themselves. They did not, for example, comfort the children after their fathers berated them but instead told them to stay away from their fathers. Yet, both the parents of both Rob and Margaret sometimes were emotionally available. They received enough sensitive, responsive care from their mothers and sometimes their fathers to seek it out with extended family members, family friends, and peers.

Rob's father was physically abusive and often hit Rob. He made fun of Rob's interests in writing, poetry, music, and drawing, saying they were girls' interests. The mother also was a well-organized homemaker, keeping the house clean, the children well-clothed, and making nourishing meals. The parents kept the family on a regular schedule for mealtimes, homework, bedtime, and waking up. The father had a steady, well-paying job. The family owned their own home in a pleasant neighborhood, where they lived since the parents were married. Both parents when to church each Sunday with the children. When Rob was a teenager, his father would ask Rob to take walks with him. Rob went because he thought he had to, but he did not enjoy himself. He would not talk to his father and would walk behind him.

Rob suffered at least two episodes of depression when he was a teenager and attempted suicide. The first time, he took all the pills in the medicine cabinet, but woke up the next day. The second time, he drove his car—that he bought with his own money—into a bridge abutment. He totaled the car but walked away without injury. Both attempts were responses to his rage and despair when his parents told him he had to break up with girlfriends they thought were not good enough for him. He obeyed them, but at great personal cost.

Rob did not feel close to anyone in his family. He said, "We never touched, and we never hugged." His mother, however, did step between him and his father when his father was hitting him. The father would stop. When Rob was thirteen, he refused to go on any more camping trips with his father, and his mother backed him up. The camping trips stopped. Rob did not did not confide in any family members, but he had other outlets for his emotions. When upset, he listened to music that soothed him. He also wrote in a diary for several years where he expressed his most private thoughts and feelings. He stopped writing when his mother read his journal and made fun of him about it.

Rob's Second Family

Rob had a life-long best friend named Pete and was a second son to the friend's parents. This family lived across the street. Rob spent as much time as he could with them. He talked freely to Pete and Pete's family about his family issues, although he did not tell them about the sexual abuse. Rob loved being with this family because they seemed to like and respect each other and liked and respected him. Rob and Pete used to take Rob's drunk father home from the bars on occasion, and Rob was home more than once with Pete when his father came home drunk. Pete simply accepted this situation and did not give Rob cause to be ashamed.

Pete's father spent a lot of time with the two boys, teaching them how to repair small appliances and motors. Rob also talked to Pete and Pete's father about relationships and how to get along with others. Rob received his sex education from his Pete's father. This man also loaned Rob money to buy a lawn mower so that Rob could set up a lawn mowing service. Rob built up a good business and expanded to clearing snow in the winter.

Rob did well in school and was a particularly good chess player. He thought he did not have enough money for college but had saved enough from his business to go to trade school where he learned to be an electrician, building on the skills and knowledge Pete's father had given him. Rob is now thirty, has a thriving electrical business, is married and has a son and daughter. He and his wife own their own home in a pleasant, residential neighborhood. Rob is active in several community organizations.

Rob's Decision

At age twenty-six, Rob realized that he had a problem. He never hit his wife, but he yelled at her loudly enough that she would become frightened and leave the home with the children to be with her parents. She used to tell him they need to get some marriage counseling but he refused. One day, after she left with the children, he saw that he had broken one of his children's toys. He then realized that he had had a tantrum, similar to the tantrums he used to hate in his own father. He cried for a long time and then phoned his wife to tell her that he would get therapy.

After a few sessions, he remembered being sexually abused. Right before the session, he had seen a television show on incest. He thought the show, in combination with the counseling, triggered memories that he had long ago put out of his mind.

He sought therapy for being a survivor of child sexual abuse, which he successfully completed. While in marriage counseling and survivor therapy, he realized that he was also physically abusive to his toddler children. He used to spank them over their diapers starting when they were less than a year old. He thought his wife was crazy when she told him that you don't hit babies. He realized how wrong he was, joined Parents Anonymous, and became a national leader in the organization. Rob had the good sense to deal with issues that troubled him and that stressed and frightened his wife and children. Had he not connected to Pete and Pete's family over a long period of time, his life could have been much different.

Emotional Development

Margaret's father was not physically abusive and was proud of her accomplishments in music, sports, and schoolwork. When he was in a good mood, he was a funny, attentive father. Margaret felt very close to her mother, older sister, and two friends whom she knew all her life from early childhood to adulthood. She could talk to her sister, mother, and friends about what was troubling her, and she often did. These family members and friends encouraged Margaret to pursue her interests and were themselves good at many things and popular with their own friends.

Professional Help

Margaret did not have major issues with depression and anxiety and had the resources to imagine a positive future and to achieve her dreams. Sexually abusing children did not cross her mind, but as a young adult, she had a series of problems with jobs and boyfriends and sought therapy for several years and then spent three years in self-help groups for adult children of alcoholics.

As a result of her participation in therapy and self-help groups, Margaret gained even more confidence in herself, went to medical school, and is a well-known academic physician, specializing in child neurology. At the age of forty-three, she has a long-term relationship with a man who is a college professor.

Both Margaret and Rob had risks for becoming perpetrators of child sexual abuse. The thought never crossed their minds. They apparently had many positive factors in their lives that helped them to overcome some of the effects of their own childhood sexual abuse and other traumas. They both had confidants and were able to express a range of emotions appropriately.

Both had many friends, did well in school, and were good at a lot of things. They did not have "me first" beliefs and typically were sensitive and responsive to others. If they were not, they usually realized it, had remorse, and apologized. They preferred connection to others and found cut-offs painful. They knew how to repair breaks in relationships.

In adulthood, both of them engaged in therapy and self-help to see themselves through to a fulfilling careers and adult lives. Wounded by childhood sexual abuse and other negative life events, they demonstrated capacities for coping with, adapting to, and overcoming adversities. They are examples of adults who show resilience.

Naïve Experimenter

The following is a case example of Maria, a woman survivor who sexually abused two toddlers she babysat when she was in her early teens. The abuse consisted of placing her leg between their thighs and pushing up. She felt guilt and shame and no sexual sensations. She never did it again. She had many protective factors in her life that helped her see that what she had done was wrong and that she had hurt the children and betrayed her own sense of herself.

At the time of her abuse, Maria said she was "numb," depressed, anxious, and alienated from her father who had sexually abused her. Her parents were upper class and prominent socially. She did not tell her mother or other adults about the sexual abuse. She thought no one would believe her because her father was so well regarded. She also was afraid she would be blamed.

Although she had many of the protective factors discussed earlier, she required therapy throughout much of her life in order to work through issues related to being an incest survivor and someone who had molested children. She might have been a life-long abuser, but she did not want to hurt children and she took steps to ensure that she did not. Maria first disclosed to her boyfriend when she was 14 that her father had sexually abused her. She also told girlfriends, her therapist in college, and her husband about the incest.

She married in her mid-twenties. She and her husband were well educated and established an upper class lifestyle themselves, including many friends, social activities, and civic engagement in terms of contributions of money and time to social welfare organizations. Yet, her husband told her, "You need help." He was concerned about her level of anxiety, her hypersensitivity, and her mood swings, although she excelled in her profession and socially. She went into therapy and joined a self-help group modeled after Alcoholics Anonymous.

After several months, Maria told her therapist about the sexual abuse she perpetrated. This became a focus of many sessions. She learned in therapy that she had made her father out to be a monster and cut herself off from him when she was a child. She said

> A big part of my surviving abuse is to make him be the bad guy. What do you do when you do the same thing?

To this day, Maria feels guilty about the abuse. She still sees the children she abused, now adults, and they are doing well in their work and family lives. She believes they were too young at the time of the abuse to remember. Maria continues her civic activities and is well-known in the region in which she lives.

Maria is a naïve experimenter who had many protective processes that helped her to never again sexually abuse children. As discussed, naïve experimenters touch children sexually once or twice and then quit. Maria required more than psychoeducation about child sexual abuse because she had many issues resulting from her own experience of incest and the generally troubled relationship she had with her father. She willingly sought treatment to work through these issues.

Discussion

These three survivors of child sexual abuse confided in other people, and in Rob's case to a diary as well, about personal, private life events. They used pro-social ways of dealing with their distress, such as listening to soothing music and talking to other people. They also did not believe that sexual contact with children was something they could do, nor did they want to. For two of them, the thought never crossed their minds. Maria acted out one time with two toddlers and was filled with guilt, shame, and remorse. She never abused again. Like Rob, some survivors have many risk factors but they also have many protective factors that offset the effects of the risks.

Others, like Maria, have fewer risks, but the risks they do have are difficult to manage. One of Maria's main risks was disgust with her father. She also realized that she was capable of doing what she hated in him, namely sexually abusing children. While some people shut down emotionally as a way of coping with emotional pain, Maria had close friends and told them her most shameful secrets beginning when she was a teenager. In her late twenties, she joined a self-help group and had intensive therapy, where she deal directly with her issues and learned new ways of managing them.

Margaret and Rob had several risks as well, but many protective factors, including being emotionally expressive, enjoying many different activities, being talented in several areas, and never having a thought about sexually abusing children.

Do sexually abused children become abusers? Most do not. They have protective factors in their lives that help them to cope with, adapt to, and overcome the effects of being sexually abused. They are emotionally expressive and do not believe that sex with children will soothe, comfort, and gratify them.

Like Margaret and Rob, most survivors do not sexually abuse children at all. If they are abusive in other ways, as Rob was, they eventually realize it and seek help. They have the resources and the will to live their lives the best way they can. They have the personal competences and emotional resources to do no harm to children. Emotionally expressive themselves, they do not believe that sex with children is a means of emotional and sexual gratification.

Some survivors may abuse children sexually one or a few times, as Maria did. It is almost as if they are trying to work out the meanings of their own trauma. Ashamed at their sexually abusive behaviors, they stop and never abuse again. As of yet, little attention is paid to people like Maria who struggle with guilt and shame for their lifetimes for a one-time incident of child sexual abuse during their teen years.

In summary, these three survivors were emotionally expressive and found comfort and meaning in their connections to others. They did not believe that are entitled to have sex with children, nor did they view sexual abuse as a source of pleasure and comfort. Persons sexually abused in childhood and who do not become abusers themselves share these characteristics.

Note: This is a chapter from *Child Sexual Abuse: From Harsh Realities to Hope,* available for Kindle, iPad, and Nook as a paperback original on Amazon.

17

Protective Factors, Resilience, and Child Abuse and Neglect
2001, slight revisions in 2012

This article discusses important concepts in prevention: protective factors, risks, resilience, dysregulation, and childhood adversities.

Slow but perceptible changes are taking place in how we think about outcomes when persons have experienced risks such as child abuse and neglect. Professionals, policy makers, and researchers are beginning to build notions of protective factors into their everyday activities. For example, health researchers now report not only on the risks for various diseases such as breast cancer and hardening of the arteries, but they also identify factors that appear to be protective against disease.

Likewise, persons concerned with childhood abuse and neglect are paying increased attention to protective factors. Though maltreatment is a serious, documented threat to the well-being and optimal development of children and adolescents, researchers and practitioners have also shown that a percentage of children and youth who have experienced abuse and neglect can function quite well (Egeland, Jacobvitz, & Sroufe, 1998; Gilgun, 1996Aa & b, 1999b; 1991, 1990; Kaufman & Zigler, 1987; Masten & Coatsworth, 1998; Widom, 1991). They are able to cope with, adapt to, or overcome the effects of maltreatment. That is, they appear to be *resilient*.

Developmental Psychopathology

Developmental psychopathologists examine patterns of human development leading both to adaptive and maladaptive outcomes by studying high risk groups, usually longitudinally (Cicchetti & Garmezy, 1993). This research has shown that not all persons with risk factors have adverse outcomes. Among the risks examined are socio-economic status, childhood maltreatment, mental health of parents, war, dangerous neighborhoods, homelessness, natural disasters, and a range of other stressors, such as illness, mother absence, family relocation, and physical punishment of children (Shields & Cicchetti, 1998; Egeland, Carlson, & Sroufe, 1993; Gilgun, Klein, & Pranis, 2000b; Richters & Martinez, 1993; Rutter, 1990; Werner & Smith, 1992).

Vulnerability and Dysregulation

When persons experience risks such as childhood abuse and neglect, they have been hurt emotionally, psychological, and sometimes physically. These hurts can be thought of as psychic wounds that may create a sense of the self as defective and helpless. Psychic wounds can lead to dysregulation, where the person at least temporarily experiences a sense of unmanageability of their thoughts, emotions, and behaviors (Shields & Cicchetti, 1998). Their autonomous nervous systems, too, may be dysregulated. Children may become anxious, fearful, aggressive, depressed, withdrawn, lethargic, hyperkinetic and show bouts of crying, sleep disturbances, bed wetting, and oppositional behaviors.

Coping with Dysregulation

When dysregulated, hurt children seek to re-regulate; that is, to regain self-efficacy, control, and mastery over themselves and their various environments (Gilgun, 2000a). Re-regulation can occur in four general ways: pro-social, anti-social, self-injurious, and inappropriate.

- *Pro-social* efforts to re-regulate include seeking comfort and affirmation from attachment figures, talking to someone about the hurt and confusion, channeling the negative affect into positive behaviors such as physical exercise and artistic expression, and seeking ways to reinterpret meanings of the hurt away from the self as bad and helpless to a sense of self as good and competent.

- *Anti-social* efforts to re-regulate include effacement and destruction of property such as destroying toys or writing on walls, picking on other people, bullying, physically attacking others, acting in sexually inappropriate ways, stealing and other oppositional behaviors. School shootings are extreme examples of young people using anti-social methods of re-regulation.
- *Self-injurious* efforts at re-regulation include cutting, anorexia, bulimia, use of drugs and alcohol, suicide attempts, recklessness, and playing with guns and other weapons.
- *Inappropriate* efforts include being silly when the mood is somber such as laughing at funerals, talking at religious services, telling jokes while a teacher is talking, and other behaviors that make sense to actors but that others experience as mystifying or disrespectful.

Protective Factors

Protective factors are resources that individuals actively use to manage, adapt to, or overcome risks. Researchers and practitioners have identified many factors that are protective for some persons under certain conditions (Cicchetti et al, 1993; Gilgun, 1999; Masten et al, 1995; Resnick, Harris, & Blum, 1993). Examples of protective factors are

- *Close, long-term relationships* with other persons who (1) model pro-social behaviors, (2) are emotionally expressive and facilitate emotional expressiveness in the at-risk person, (3) praise and encourage pro-social behaviors in the at-risk person, (4) know and understand the risks experienced by the at-risk person and maintain closeness when the complexity of these risks is disclosed;
- A *confidant(e)* whom the at-risk person makes efforts to emulate, and with whom s/he reciprocates a sense of closeness, seeks support and counsel during times of stress and fear, and freely shares painful personal issues;
- A *strong desire to be pro-social*, including appropriate emotional expressiveness and a determination to do well;

- *A favorable sense of self* that challenges images of the self as bad and powerlessness;
- *The ability to engage in self-soothing behaviors;* for example listening to music, engaging in affirming self-talk, and imagining a fulfilling future;
- *An affirming ethnic and cultural identification;*
- *Hope* for a more positive future, along with the capacity to imagine a positive future and seeking and using resources that help build toward that positive future.

No one factor is likely to be protective against the many adversities that children and youth may have experienced. However, a combination of the factors listed above are associated with persons overcoming, coping, and adapting to risks. Stable long-term relationships are central because of the "hot buttons" associated with vulnerability; when the hot buttons are stimulated, at-risk persons who cope well seek confidant(e)s to help them work through their dysregulation. Confidant(e)s can be parents, other adults within or outside of families, siblings, and peers.

When young people identify with and want to be like pro-social people, when they confide in people who help them to cope in prosocial ways and challenge any anti-social beliefs they have internalized, and when the children themselves reject antisocial and inappropriate ways of self-regulation, then young people are at low risk to develop antisocial behaviors.

Not all antisocial behaviors, however, are linked to dysregulation and experiences of child abuse and neglect. The single factor that appears in all forms of violence, regardless of abuse and neglect status, are beliefs that it is okay and even desirable to engage in violent acts to get what you want and to feel better. In short, many people who use violence have not experienced abuse and neglect and most people who have experienced abuse and neglect do not commit violent acts. Several articles in this book demonstrate this principle.

Resilience

Resilience is a process that occurs over time. Many types of resources in many different settings over time promote resilience in children and youth. This requires on-going, affirming relationships that guide young people toward self-efficacy, pro-sociality, and self-regulation. Persons can be considered resilient when they demonstrate capacities for coping with, adapting to, and overcoming risks and can re-establish or maintain their equilibrium when "hot buttons" are pushed. Resilience is not an all or nothing process. Persons can be resilient in somesituations and be overcome with vulnerabilities in others (Gilgun, 1999).

Overcoming the odds is difficult. To do so, young persons must want to overcome adversities in pro-social ways. Adults, in our roles as parents, policy makers, program planners, prevention specialists, and direct practitioners, have the task of providing resources that children and youth recognize as important to them and are consistent with what they want. The most valuable resources are time and attention that eventually result in young persons' increasing capacities to regulate and re-regulate themselves in times of stress.

References

Cicchetti, Dante & Norman Garmezy (1993). Editorial: Prospects and promises in the study of resilience. *Development and Psychopathology, 5*, 497-502.

Cicchetti, Dante, Fred A. Rogosch, Michael Lynch, & Kathleeen D. Holt (1993). Resilience in maltreated children: Processes leading to adaptive outcomes. *Development and Psychopathology, 5*, 629-647.

Egeland, Byron, E. Carlson, Elizabeth, & L. Alan Sroufe (1993). Resilience as process. *Development and Psychopathology, 5*, 517-528.

Egeland, Byron, Deborah Jacobvitz, & L. Alan Sroufe (1988). Breaking the cycle of abuse. *Child Development, 59*, 1080-1088.

Gilgun, Jane F. (2000a, June). A Comprehensive Theory of Interpersonal Violence, paper presented at the paper presented at the conference on the Victimization of Children and Youth: An International Research Conference, Durham, NH, June 25-28.

Gilgun, Jane F. Christian Klein, & Kay Pranis. (2000b). The significance of resources in models of risk, *Journal of Interpersonal Violence, 14*, 627-646.

Gilgun, Jane F. (1999). Mapping resilience as process among adults maltreated in childhood. In Hamilton I. McCubbin, Elizabeth A. Thompson, Anne I. Thompson, & Jo A. Futrell (Eds.), *The dynamics of resilient families.* (pp. 41-70). Thousand Oaks, CA: Sage.

Gilgun, Jane F. (1996a). Human development and adversity in ecological perspective: Part 1: A conceptual framework. *Families in Society, 77*, 395-402.

Gilgun, Jane F. (1996b). Human development and adversity in ecological perspective, Part 2: Three patterns. *Families in Society, 77*, 459-576.

Gilgun, Jane F. (1991). Resilience and the intergenerational transmission of child sexual abuse. In Michael Q. Patton (Ed.), *Family sexual abuse: Frontline research and evaluation* (pp. 93-105). Newbury Park, CA: Sage.

Gilgun, Jane F. (1990). Factors mediating the effects of childhood maltreatment. In Mic Hunter (Ed.), *The sexually abused male: Prevalence, impact, and treatment* (pp. 177-190). Lexington, MA: Lexington Books.

Kaufman, Joan , & Edward Zigler (1987). Do abused children become abusive parents? *American Journal of Orthopsychiatry, 57*, 186-192.

Masten, Ann S. (1994). Resilience in individual development: Successful adaptation despite risk and adversity. In M. C. Wang & E. W. Gordon (Eds.), *Educational resilience in Inner-city America: Challenges and prospects* (pp. 3-23). Hillsdale, NJ: Erlbaum.

Masten, Ann. S., & J. Douglas Coatsworth (1998). The development of competence in favorable and unfavorable environments: Lessons from research on successful children. *American Psychologist, 53*, 205-220.

Masten, Ann S., Karin M. Best & Norman Garmezy (1991). Resilience and development: Contributions from the study of children who overcome adversity. *Development and Psychopathology, 2*, 425-444.

Resnick, Michael. D., L. J. Harris, & Robert W. Blum (1993). The impact of caring and connectedness on adolescent health and well-being. *Journal of Pediatrics and Child Health, 29,* *suppl.1,* 53-59.

Richters, John E. & Pedro E. Martinez (1993). Violent communities, family choices, and children's chances: An algorithm for improving the odds. *Development and Psychopathology, 5,* 609-627.

Rutter, Michael. (1990). Commentary: Some focus and process considerations regarding effects of parental depression on children. *Developmental Psychology, 26,* 60-67.

Shields, Ann & Dante Cicchetti (1998). Reactive aggression among maltreated children: The contributions of attention and emotion dysregulation. *Journal of Clinical Child Psychology, 27,* 381-395.

Werner, Emme E., & Ruth S. Smith (1992). *Overcoming the odds: High risk children from birth to adulthood.* Ithaca, N.Y.: Cornell University Press.

Widom, Cathy Spatz (1991). Avoidance of criminality in abused and neglected children. *Psychiatry, 54,* 162-174.

Part 3: Accountability

18

Evil Feels Good: Think Before You Act

Some people don't intend to hurt others, or at least they are thinking more about the consequences for themselves and don't think about the effects of their actions on others. In this article, a college student wanted to have fun and be the center of attention. He didn't think about the consequences for the young man who was the target of his "fun." This articles gives some suggestions about how to think before you act and then what to do if you hurt someone without really meaning to—in other words, how to be accountable.

The funny thing about evil is that it feels good when we do it. That's why it's so hard for us to recognize evil when we commit it. People who do evil think a lot of different things, most of them pleasant and even compelling to themselves.

A case in point is the actions of an 18-year-old New Jersey college student who secretly videotaped his roommate being intimate with another man in their dorm room and then posting the video on the Internet. On September 19, 2010, he wrote on Twitter, "Roommate asked for room until midnight. I went into molly's room and turned on my webcam. I saw him making out with a dude. Yay."

A few days later on September 22, the videotaped young man jumped off the George Washington Bridge. The police found his body nine days later. The day he jumped, he left a message on Facebook that read, "Jumping off the gw bridge sorry."

The young man who videotaped posted a Twitter message the day before the suicide, "Anyone with iChat, I dare you to video chat me between the hours of 9:30 and 12. Yes, it's happening again."

This was fun for the man who did the videotaping and then made it available on the internet. It was the end of the world for the young man who was videotaped.

Evil as Sport

The chair of a gay rights group said, "We are sickened that anyone in our society…might consider destroying others' lives as a sport."

The young man who videotaped did make a sport out of someone else's intimacies. He may have thought that gay baiting is a legitimate sport. Plenty of people believe that. I think he was caught up in the fun of posting the videotape. He probably thought the video would be funny for many other people. It may have been. I do not think he meant to destroy a life. I do not think he thought that far ahead.

Now It's Too Late

The man who videotaped is not having fun anymore. The police charged him with two counts of invasion of privacy, which carries a maximum penalty of five years in prison. Some are calling for hate crime charges that have severe penalties, too. His university expelled him.

This young man did not think that his roommate would be so hurt that he would kill himself. He thought no further than the fun he was having. If it's fun, do it. That's what guided him.

Evil Actions do Not Fit Stereotypes

Like others who do evil, the man who videotaped had the respect of friends and the love of his family. Students from the high school where he had graduated in June described him as kind and from a loving family. He was voted "best dancer." His parents took out an ad in the yearbook that read in part, "It has been a pleasure watching you grow into a caring and responsible person."

This brief portrait shows that we can't rely on stereotypes to identify people who do evil acts. Most people who do great harm to others do not have pencil thin mustaches, slick-backed hair, staring eyes, and wear a cloak that they use to cover the lower part of their faces. They look like you and me.

Consequences and Evil

Some of the students at the university where the crime occurred debated whether the man's actions were a thoughtless prank or a heinous crime. Evil acts are not usually evil in intent. People who commit great harm set out to have a good time or to satisfy some desire for wholeness and pleasure. Evil acts such as uploading a video of private acts are in the minds of actors harmless pranks, but in the consequences they are heinous crimes.

Consequences show whether actions are evil or not. Intentions mean nothing when another person is greatly harmed.

Civility Training

The university that the two young men attended had been planning civility training to prevent hurtful uses of technology and group psychology. The training starting just days ago. This incident gave renewed energy for the training to a dazed and traumatized student body.

Accountability Training

The university might consider accountability training. Most people would undo the hurt they cause. After all, they did not mean to hurt anyone in the first place. They had been selfish and thought only of themselves. Such persons, and this is pretty much all of us, need pointers on how to make up for what they have done. They know they have lost the respect of people who are important to them.

Here are some things we can do.

- **Admit it.** State clearly and completely what you did.

- **Describe effects of your actions on the people you hurt.** Be clear and concise, but give details on how your actions affected others.
- **Take complete responsibility.** Do not make jokes, blame others, or plead extenuating circumstances. After all, you did do it.
- **Say you are sorry and mean it.** As you speak, notice whether you actually do feel sorry. If you do not, you are not being accountable.
- **Accept recrimination.** Listen and hear what the people you have harmed have to say about your actions.
- **Do not repeat your harmful actions,** no matter how good you think these actions will make you feel. Statements of accountability and apology mean nothing if you turn right around and hurt others once again.

If we do this, we may earn our way back into the good graces of people who have lost respect for us because of our harmful actions. If people respect you because you committed harmful acts, then you may have to re-think whether you want that kind of respect. What kind of person are you?

If it Feels Good, Think

The lesson to be learned is, that if it feels good, think ahead before you act. Ask, will this hurt anyone? What is the worst case scenario? What is the best case scenario? For the persons I may hurt? For myself? For my family? For my friends? For the other person's family? For the other person's friends?

The family of the man who committed suicide said, he "was a fine young man and a distinguished musician. The family is heartbroken beyond words."

19

It's Time for the Roman Catholic Church to Show the World What Penitence is

I thought I had heard the worst of it, but then a Roman Catholic bishop in Canada just went to prison for child pornography. In this article, I point out that most clergy live exemplary lives, but I also point out that the church has protected thousands of child molesters and overlooked the terrible harm these priests have caused. I suggest that the Roman Catholic Church become a world-wide model of penitence.

Just when I thought I had seen the worst of it, I read about the imprisonment of Raymond Lahey, former Roman Catholic bishop of Antigonish, Canada. Yesterday, Bishop Lahey pled guilty to one charge of child pornography. He immediately began to serve a year in prison.

Mr. Lahey got off easy. Canadian border officials discovered on his laptop almost 600 photos of boys in degrading sexual poses, videos, and stories about boys having sex with each other. His passport showed he had visited Thailand, Malaysia, and Indonesia, hotspots for men seeking sex with children. Mr. Lahey denied an interest in boys, but said he was attracted to older males. Whatever happened to his promise of celibacy? How about decency? Respect? The life of Jesus he had publicly espoused?

The Roman Catholic Church, like other religious institutions, has been a force for good for more than two thousands years. Every religious organization, as far as I know, teaches the faithful to love one another, to uphold the dignity and worth of other human beings, and to stand for social justice. Most of the women and men who dedicate themselves to the religious life have lived exemplary lives and have done untold good.

At the same time, this church has created an institution where thousands of their priests, consecrated as they are to God, betray the values that the church stands for. The record is clear on this church's history of protecting and covering up the terrible deeds of pedophiles and other priests who exploit parishioners sexually.

Those in charge of the Roman Catholic Church have an unprecedented opportunity to show the world what penitence is. I would like the Roman Catholic Church to do an examination of conscience and then to reform itself. This is what their priests tell the faithful to do. So must they. To do this, each member of the Roman Catholic clergy and laity has to be skeptical of her or his relationship with God.

An Examination of Conscience

From early childhood, the Roman Catholic Church teaches its members that we are sinners and we must identify our sins, experience sorrow for the harm we have caused, confess what we have done, be accountable for what we have done, do penance, and then to take measures that ensure that we do not keep on harming others. When church members do this, we have meaningful lives.

The administrators of the Roman Catholic Church must do the same. Priests, bishops, cardinals, and the pope are sinners. It is not just parishioners who sin. Those who are priests must examine their own consciences in regard to the sexual abuse clergy has committed. This examination of conscience would have several parts. Each part would contribute to what could be a fairly complete picture of what has gone wrong to permit the abuse to happen and what goes right when priests and other religious live exemplary lives.

This examination of conscience can begin with seeking to understand the lives of the priests who have committed sexual abuse. These priests would tell their life stories to well-trained interviewers. Each priest would be interviewed many times until they are satisfied that they have told their life stories as honestly as they can. I have done this kind of research with perpetrators and survivors of child sexual abuse for many years.

It is amazing how grateful people are to have someone listen to them as they share the truth of their lives. It does not seem to matter whether the truth is something they are proud of or not. There is something deeply meaningful about the telling. I expect that many of these priests would be grateful for the opportunity, would express deep sorrow, and seek ways to make up for what they have done. The act of participating in the interviews is a way for penitent priests to make up for the harm they have caused. Such interviews would include members of religious orders who are not priests but are brothers as well as lay members of religious orders who have abused others sexually.

An examination of conscience would also involve life histories of priests who have not sexually abused children and who, according to nominations from parishioners, have been exemplary priests. We need these interviews in order to discern what has gone right and what has gone wrong in the lives of men who have publicly declared themselves to be followers of Jesus and desirous of helping others be followers of Jesus.

The women of the church who have dedicated themselves to following Jesus as nuns and members of lay religious orders would also be sources of ideas about the nature of exemplary lives and the conditions that have allowed so many pedophile priests to operate within the Roman Catholic Church.

Some of these religious women may have been sexually abusive to church members. They, like the male priests and brothers, may want to tell their life stories as ways of making up for the harm they have caused. As with priests, most of them have lived exemplary lives. From understanding the conditions under which individuals live exemplary lives can come principles that may guide others to do the same.

An examination of conscience would also involve interviews with priests, including bishops, archbishops, cardinals, and the pope, about their personal experiences with priests who have sexually abused children and other parishioners. This, too, would involve multiple interviews over time. As with the priests who were active sexual abusers, at least some of those who had responsibility for supervising them are likely to want to share their stories, express their sorrow, and seek ways to make up for what they have done or not done.

Furthermore, an examination of conscience would involve interviews with survivors of priest sexual abuse, their families, and parishioners in general. The number of interviews would vary depending upon the depths to which these persons would want to go and how much and what they want to say. Many of these people might have excellent ideas about what went wrong and how the Roman Catholic Church can correct these wrongs.

Another step in an examination of conscience is to interview religious leaders and theologians within the Roman Catholic Church and members of other faiths to gather ideas about what they think may have gone wrong with a church that permitted such wide-spread abuse. These individuals, too, might have some ideas about how the Roman Catholic Church can correct these wrongs and the conditions under which individuals live exemplary lives.

Theologians may have insight into the importance of being skeptical about our relationship with God, the importance of doubting whether we really are following God's will, and the centrality of allowing others to know what is in our hearts so that they can help us not fool ourselves into thinking we are following God's will when we are not. I discuss skepticism about our relationship with God later in this article.

It is hard to anticipate what kinds of issues will surface through these interviews, both in terms of what went wrong and what the remedies might be, or are worth trying. Yet, I can think of no other way for the Roman Catholic Church to make up for these terrible deeds without this wide-spread examination of conscience.

The interviewers would be well trained to listen and to create a sense of safety so that the persons they interview feel safe and respected. The interviewers should also be from a variety of religious faiths and be trained in the best traditions of social science research. This means they continually examine themselves and each other for biases that might distort what interviewees might want to say. There are standard procedures for researchers to ensure that they deal with their biases.

The results of these interviews would be disseminated in every possible way. These ways include press releases, internet publications, scholarly journals, textbooks, religious education including courses on theology, in the confessional, and through preaching from the pulpit. What ought to come through clearly is the recognition of the deep harm sexual abuse has caused so many, sincere sorrow for the harm, and heartfelt requests for forgiveness.

Those harmed may not want to extend forgiveness in the sense of saying "It's all in the past; it's time to move on." Most will say, "I feel sorry that you cloaked yourself in virtue and took advantage of me. I let go of my hurt and guilt. I did nothing wrong. I hope your penitence is sincere. I want nothing to do with you. I want to surround myself with people who love me more than they love their own sexual and emotional gratification."

Reform

Based on what these interviews might show, the Roman Catholic Church would have a wealth of ideas about how to make up for the terrible deeds that some of their priests have perpetrated and that the structures, procedures, and unstated assumptions of the Church have allowed.

I believe that the principles of accountability, penance, contrition, and reform are already present in the minds and hearts of persons of the faithful. I hope that the administrators of the Roman Catholic Church have the foresight to tap into this wisdom.

The values on which the Roman Catholic Church stands are a powerful force for good. The kind of examination of conscience that I suggest would result in a compilation of wisdom that would not only renew the Church but be a worldwide model of accountability.

Skepticism

I believe that those who perpetrate child sexual abuse had no doubt that their sexual acts were good, not only for themselves but for the children and others they abused. Priests who believe sexual abuse is good obviously do not consider that they may be fooling themselves about God's will for them. They do not have the doubts and skepticism that I believe is inseparable from faith.

I have conducted interviews with perpetrators of child sexual abuse for more than 25 years. With some exceptions, these perpetrators experienced these sexual behaviors as good. They experienced what they thought was intimacy, bliss, the greatest feelings of the world, joy, completeness. In their own minds, what they did was not sexual abuse. The following is a sample of what perpetrators say.

Christian, in his early fifties, described the sexual abuse of his 13 year-old stepson, Seth, as a love affair.

> I didn't call it molesting. It was making love to my son....When I was having my relationship with my son it was like a love affair. It really was. It was real.

He continued.

> What I was doing was different. I was making love to my daughter, to my son.

Joe said

> We never had penile intercourse. I don't know why. I had it stuck in my brain that I couldn't have that. That was incest to me.

In addition, some abusers are outraged when they hear about other instances of child sexual abuse. Mike said

> I used to sit there and watch TV or I'd read something in the paper. I'd say, 'Look at this son of a bitch. He ought to get twenty years,' but I was doing the same thing. Mine wasn't that way. See, mine was love. There's a difference, you know.

Roger Vangheluwe, former Roman Catholic Bishop of Bruges, Belgium, experienced child sexual abuse as "a certain kind of intimacy that took place." He elaborated on this statement on live French television during the fifth week on Lent in 2011.

I have often been involved with children, and I never felt the slightest attraction. It was a certain kind of intimacy that took place.

I don't have the impression at all that I am a pedophile. It was really just a small relationship. I did not have the feeling that my nephew was against it—quite the contrary.

How did it begin? As with all families, when they came to visit, the nephews slept with me. It began as a game with the boys. It was never a question of rape. There was never any physical violence used. He never saw me naked, and there was no penetration.

I believe that the bishop is speaking the truth as he experienced it. He did not believe that what he did was anything other than intimacy and that he did not harm his nephew.

Some might argue that the men who perpetrate child sexual abuse are misguided. That they are, but what about the priests who had dedicated themselves to God? What about the bishop of Bruges? The bishop in Canada? These men had dedicated their lives to God. The bishops had been consecrated as bishops.

Priests are supposed to examine their consciences and consult with a spiritual advisor or a confessor to make sure they are was fulfilling their promise of living holy lives. They promised to be celibate, meaning no sex with anyone. I believe that priests who committed sexual abuse mistook evil for good. There has to be some mechanism within the Roman Catholic Church that permits this mistaking of evil for good. Many priests have done exactly what the Bishop of Bruges and the Canadian bishop have done. They must believe that their evil acts are good.

There has to be a mechanism or set of assumptions in the Roman Catholic Church that permits some priests to believe that they are consecrated to God and therefore can not do wrong. Certainly, most priests do not believe they can do no wrong. Most priests believe themselves to be sinners along with the rest of us.

A few do not believe they are sinners. Some are likely to believe that the sexual abuse they perpetrate is a form of God's love. Survivors have said that priests who abused them have said this.

Such priests are not skeptical enough of their relationship with God. Human beings see through the glass darkly. It is difficult to discern God's will for us. We have to be full of doubt about God's will and consult openly and honestly with others when we are about to undertake an action, especially an action that involves others.

Imagine how differently today's Roman Catholic Church would be if every priest who has committed sexual abuse first consulted with a spiritual advisor. Imagine if these priests had openly and honestly said they believe that what they want to do is a manifestation of God's love. I believe their spiritual advisors would have guided them to think more deeply and widely about the actions they wanted to take.

Somehow, these priests who committed child sexual abuse had so much pride in their special relationship with God that they did not question themselves when they thought about and then acted out sexually with children and other parishioners. I wonder if they believed they had a right to fulfill their sexual fantasies.

I believe that they believed they were acting out God's love. Maybe not all of them, but a lot of them did. Some of them may have realized they have harmed children and other parishioners.

One More Thing

If the Roman Catholic priestly hierarchy do not believe that examinations of conscience as I suggest, reform, and skepticism about God's will compose a plan they would like to follow, then I suggest internet surveys that anyone who is internet savvy can do.

The following are some questions for the survey.

1. how many of survivors of clergy abuse received an apology from the priests who abused them?

2. if they did receive apologies, did these survivors experience these priests as understanding the harm they had caused?

3. if survivors felt as if anybody in the Roman Catholic Church cared about the abuse they experienced;

4. if they ever felt it was safe to talk to anyone about sexual contact or attempted sexual contact with clergy and other religious;

5. if they are afraid to talk to anyone in the Roman Catholic Church out of fear of being blamed for their own abuse;

6. if they believe the abuse is their fault;

7. if they feel dirty because of the abuse;

8. if the Roman Catholic Church ever offered them opportunities to share their experiences with clergy abuse for the purpose of helping the church to understand the nature of abuse.

These are sample questions that would be important to ask. Survivors would benefit from opportunities to share their experiences this way.

Discussion

Examinations of conscience, reform, and skepticism are the kinds of steps the Roman Catholic Church could take in order to make up for the terrible deeds that some members of their clergy have committed. The Roman Catholic Church must do an examination of conscience. The Roman Catholic Church must reform itself based upon what it learns from this examination of conscience. All human beings, including priests, must be skeptical of any special relationship they think they have with God.

Not only would such actions help heal uncounted hundreds of thousands of hurt parishioners throughout the world, but such actions would also be a model of how to do atone for terrible deeds and to make things right.

If the Roman Catholic Church does not want to take these steps, then anyone can post a survey on the internet and start gathering much-needed information.

Final Note

A May 4, 2011 statement from Anthony Mancini, Archbishop of Halifax and Apostolic Administrator of the Diocese of Yarmouth, assured his audience that Raymond Lahey, the former bishop, will be dealt with by the church. He also asked people not to want revenge but forgiveness. The Archbishop did not address the deep wounds and harm that Raymond Lahey had caused. This is one more example of the need for an examination of conscience in the Roman Catholic Church.

Sexual abuse results in soul wounds that affect the quality of life and life chances of survivors. It is time for the administrators of the Church to acknowledge this and to take all means possible to ensure it does not happen to one more person, child, teenager or adult. Such steps involve a humble, thorough examination of the forces that led to such massive hurt to so many within an institution that is supposed to do good. The world is in need of a model of repentance and reform. The Roman Catholic Church is positioned to offer such a gift.

References

Blanchfield, Mike (2011). Roman Catholic bishop Raymond Lahey pleads guilty to child-porn charge. The Canadian Press, May 5. http://www.google.com/hostednews/canadianpress/article/ALeqM5hxAG5f25LDTWM3w0wFVG2DBi7eRQ?docId=6750634

Castle, Stephanie & Rachel Donadio (2011). Bishop in sexual abuse case prompts new outrage in Belgium. New York Times, April 16, p. A4.

Gilgun, Jane F. (2011). By all means, do not renounce Satan and his evil works. http://www.scribd.com/doc/52492534/By-All-Means-Do-Not-Renounce-Satan-and-his-Evil-Works

Gilgun, Jane F. (2011). Perfect: The bishop has no shame. Chapter in present book. http://www.amazon.com/Perfect-Bishop-Violence-Change-ebook/dp/B004WT7FYY/ref=sr_1_3?s=digital-text&ie=UTF8&qid=1348866996&sr=1-3&keywords=Jane+Gilgun+the+bishop

Gilgun, Jane F. (2010). *Child sexual abuse: From harsh realities to hope.* Amazon, Kindle, iBooks, Scribd, & Nook.

Gilgun, Jane F. (2010). Evil feels good: Think before you act. Chapter in present book. http://www.amazon.com/s/ref=nb_sb_noss?url=search-alias%3Daps&field-keywords=Jane+Gilgun+evil+feels+good

Gilgun, Jane F. (2010). Fake accountability & true: Telling the difference. Chapter in present book. http://www.amazon.com/True-Fake-Accountabilility-Difference-ebook/dp/B0044XUVBC/ref=sr_1_1?s=digital-text&ie=UTF8&qid=1348867513&sr=1-1&keywords=Jane+Gilgun+fake

Gilgun, Jane F. (2010). *On being a shit: Unkind deeds and cover-ups in everyday life.* Amazon, Kindle, iBooks, & Nook.

Gilgun, Jane F. (2010). Survivors of priest abuse told for 50 years: No one listened. http://www.amazon.com/Survivors-Priest-Abuse-Years-ebook/dp/B003E7FWB8/ref=sr_1_3?s=digital-text&ie=UTF8&qid=1348867586&sr=1-3&keywords=Jane+Gilgun+survivors

Gilgun, Jane F. (2010). Why they do it: Beliefs & emotional gratification lead to violent acts. Chapter in present book. http://www.amazon.com/s/ref=nb_sb_noss?url=search-alias%3Daps&field-keywords=Jane+Gilgun+why+they+do+it

The Diocese of Antigonish. http://www.antigonishdiocese.com/title.htm? Statements regarding Raymond J. Lahey, former bishop of Antigonish, may be found at: The Canadian Conference of Catholic Bishops ?http://www.cccb.ca/site/eng?

The Vatican Press Office http://www.vatican.va/news_services/press/vis/vis_en.html

Afterword

The following is an example of what the pope and abusive priests can say. This is an excerpt from "Survivors of Priest Abuse Told for 50 Years: No one Listened."

Pope Benedict's Opportunity

In the past several years, Pope Benedict has changed. He has learned that past Church policy was wrong. He has made many statements to that effect. He has expressed concern to survivors in personal meetings with them. He has said that Church actions of the past are shameful. Many, like me, do not think he has gone far enough, but he has come to realize that past policy led to hurts and wrongs.

Most religions are compassionate. We are taught to love the sinner but not the sin. We are taught to confess, to be fully accountable for our wrong-doings, to be contrite, to do penance, and to change our ways.

By his actions, Pope Benedict is a sinner along with the rest of us. He has an opportunity to be an international role model of accountability. He can make a full public confession of his sins on the steps of St. Peter's Church, in Rome, where he is the pastor. This is an example of what he can say.

I have been wrong about the sexual abuse of children. I have shown callous disregard for the well-being of children. I have allowed archbishops, bishops, cardinals, and other priests to show callous disregard for children. These actions are wrong. Sacrificing children for the sake of the Church's reputation is wrong. Showing mercy to abusing priests without accountability is wrong. I have committed grievous sins.

Child sexual abuse is an abuse of power. When priests sexually abuse children, they take advantage of Church teachings that priests are God's representatives on Earth. Children believe this. Priests tell children that sexual abuse is God's love and God wants children to learn about love and to be loving. This is a hideous distortion of Church teachings. Abusing priests have distorted Church teachings so that they can experience what they believe are the greatest feelings in the world, states of bliss and fulfillment, and bliss.

I have allowed priests to take advantage of children even after I learned that they were sexual abusers of children. I hope the Church faithful can forgive me. The faithful will see that every action I take from now on in regard to priest sexual abuse will be to show compassion for survivors and to make every human effort to prevent any child sexual abuse in the future.

The Pope can also advise cardinals, archbishops, bishops, and other priests who have been involved in protecting the Church and showing disregard for children to make similar public statements of accountability.

In addition, the Pope can institute policies where priests who have abused children in the past and any who are discovered to have sexually abused children to make full confessions on the steps of St. Peter's. This is an example of what these priests can say.

I was selfish and insensitive. I took advantage of my position as a priest. The children believed I was special. They believed I was God's representative on earth. The children were afraid to say no to me. I hurt them. I am sorry. I will do whatever I have to do to make sure I do not hurt any other children again. I abused my power. I knew deep down I had power over children and they would do what I wanted.

I did not care what the children wanted. I wanted the incredible pleasure I got from sexually abusing children. What children wanted and needed from me did not matter. All that mattered was what I wanted. I fooled myself into believing the children enjoyed the sex, but in my heart I knew better. The children wanted me to love then, but not in sexual ways. Children required my fond regard and guidance and not exploitation. Whatever abuse I experienced in the past is not excuse for my own abuse.

I betrayed my priestly vows. I am sorry. I will do whatever it takes to make up for the hurt I have caused. By my acts of sexual abuse, I have shown callous disregard for the welfare of children.

A Fairy Tale?

Are public statements of wrong-doings a fairy tale? A fantasy? Do the Pope, others responsible for not protecting children, and abusing priest truly believe Church doctrine? If they do, they will make full public confessions that are broadcast throughout the world. Showing how to be accountable can have an enormous impact for good.

20

Did Something Wrong? Admit it & Take the Consequences

When you do something wrong, promptly admit it. You will be glad you did. This article gives examples of people who did wrong or are accused of doing wrong. It shows the consequences of admitting and denying alleged wrongdoing. Everyone makes mistakes. Everyone hurts others. Here are suggestions about what to do about it.

When you do something wrong, why not just admit it, take the consequences, and get on with your life? Let other people get on with theirs? Two people in the news did just that. One person said he did it, he's sorry, won't do it again, and won't forget what he did. This person is Joakim Noah, a professional basketball player, who called a fan a "fucking faggot" during a game. Noah took responsibility for his misdeed. He got a lot of heat for the slur and accepted widespread disapproval.

The other person is Molly Wei, 19, charged in crimes related to the death of Tyler Clementi, 18, a first year college student at Rutgers University in New Jersey, USA. Mr. Clementi committed suicide last fall, days after his roommate, Dharun Ravi, 19, posted a video of Mr. Clementi making out with another man. Ms. Wei struck a deal with prosecutors.

In exchange for a guilty plea, 300 hours of community service, successful completion of counseling, and truthful testimony in Mr. Ravi's trial, all charges against her will be dropped. Ms. Wei faces charges of invasion of privacy because Mr. Ravi was in her room when he turned on the webcam to videotape Mr. Clementi and his date.

Who Me? Never!

Two other people in the news won't admit what they did. Under US law, they assumed to be innocent until they are proved guilty through trial. In this article, I wonder what would happen if they did what they were charged with and then simply admitted it.

These two people are charged with crimes. One of them, the former head of the International Monetary Fund (IMF), denied raping a hotel maid 30 years his junior a few weeks ago. This woman is a political refugee who has asylum in the United States. She is raising a 15 year-old daughter.

In his letter of resignation as director of the IMF, Dominique Strauss-Kahn, 62, denied "with the greatest possible firmness all of the allegations." A few days later, his lawyer stated in court, "The forensic evidence, we believe, is not consistent with a forcible encounter." This statement implicitly blames the victim. Many people do. Maybe this defense will work for Mr. Strauss-Kahn.

The other person who stated he is not guilty is Dharun Ravi, 19, who is alleged to have videotaped his male roommate making out with another man, posted the video on the web, and then allegedly wrote on Twitter, "Roommate asked for the room till midnight. I went into Molly's room and turned on my webcam. I saw him making out with a dude. Yay."

Ravi was having fun. Some of his friends thought what he did was hilarious.

Mr. Ravi's roommate. Tyler Clementi, 18, jumped to his death off the George Washington Bridge in New York City a few days later. Mr. Clementi is thought to have written a message on a gay website the day before he committed suicide. He said he told a resident advisor about the posting of the video. "I feel like it was 'look at what a fag my roommate is,'" he wrote. He said Ravi's friends showed more concern about Ravi having a gay roommate than about Ravi's actions.

Mr. Ravi pled not guilty yesterday in a Manhattan court to 15 counts of criminal behavior. These counts included bias crimes, tampering with witnesses, and tampering with evidence. Besides the spying, the posting, the bragging, and in general having a great time, Mr. Ravi afterward tried to erase his Twitter message and asked witnesses to change their stories.

Consequences

As Mr. Clementi said, actions have consequences. This is what has resulted from the actions of these four people.

Mr. Noah

The National Basketball Association (NBA) fined Mr. Noah $50,000 for the use of "a derogatory and offensive term." Mr. Noah said, "With the comment to the fan, I just want to apologize for that. I had just picked up my second foul. I was frustrated. He said something that was disrespectful toward me, and I lost my cool. People who know me know I'm an open-minded guy. I'm not here to hurt anybody's feelings."

People across the United States had a lot to say about Mr. Noah's use of a slur against gay people. For instance, the president of the Human Rights Campaign said, "We need to get to the point where you don't use an antigay slur to respond to events." A spokesperson for the Gay and Lesbian Alliance Against Defamation said, "Last month, the NBA sent an important message about how such slurs fuel a climate of intolerance and are unacceptable."

Last month the NBA fined Kobe Bryant, another basketball player, $100,000 for using the same slur against a referee.

Mr. Noah seems sincere in his apology. His subsequent actions will show whether he has learned to root out antigay attitudes that he and many others have encoded in their brains. Few people do not. We are exposed over our lifetimes to antigay beliefs.

Mr. Ravi

Mr. Ravi faces months if not years of ordeal that includes public scrutiny and disgrace. He could easily improve his reputation and, more importantly, his self respect, if he admitted what he did was wrong and took the consequences, if he did break laws.

Judges look favorably upon defendants who do this. Mr. Ravi could serve some jail time and then probation. Other people will respect that he made some terrible mistakes, but he has also understood the gravity of what he did. He can make up for his misdeeds through living an exemplary life. Admitting what he did was wrong might also relieve some of the loss and suffering that he has caused Mr. Clementi's parents, other family members, and friends.

Instead, Mr. Ravi has chosen to fight the charges, continue to damage his reputation and self-respect, and risk being found guilty and then sentenced to years in prison. He has chosen yet another self-destructive path. Amusing himself at Mr. Clementi's expense, while destructive to others, ultimately was destructive to himself.

Mr. Strauss-Kahn

Mr. Strauss-Kahn has experienced world-wide disgrace and loss of a high profile job, although many people in his native France believe his defense and think his political enemies set him up. Mr. Strauss-Kahn was a probable candidate for president of France. His great job is over and his influential future may be in doubt.

Had Mr. Strauss-Kahn admitted what he had done (if the charges are correct, although he remains innocent under the law), the headlines would not roll out every day. He would not have been photographed in handcuffs with his head lowered and his face in a scowl. The story would have made news, but it would be over by now. As discussed earlier, judges look favorably upon defendants who admit what they have done. Mr. Strauss-Kahn may have served minimal jail time and probation.

He would have earned the respect of others. "I made a mistake," he could have said. "I am sorry. I will do whatever I can to make up for what I did. I lost my head." He also could have admitted that he thought the woman was easy pickings. They were alone in the hotel room. He is far bigger than her. He perceived her as vulnerable not only because of her size but because of her dark skin and implicit "social inferiority" as compared to his high social standing.

Had he admitted what he did (innocent as he remains under the law), the 32 year-old hotel maid might have felt as if someone recognized what she had gone through, not only as a result of the sexual aggression she said she experienced from Mr. Strauss-Kahn, but also as a refugee from a worn-torn country.

She has not been public about the trauma she experienced in her country of origin. Because she is a political refugee, she has experienced multiple traumas. Women who are members of ethnic minority groups are at risk for sexual assault because of widespread beliefs about their social inferiority.

If Mr. Strauss-Kahn did act in sexually aggressive ways, he may yet restore the respect of others if , "I acted like a pig. I tried to take advantage of a situation. I need to start thinking differently about what I think I'm entitled to. I have had a life of privilege. I have to learn to know when I take advantage of people. I have gotten away with taking advantage of others for a long time." I doubt that Mr. Strauss-Kahn has suffered any pain over damage to his self-respect. He could truly believe he is not guilty.

Ms. Wei

Ms. Wei will be able to go on with her life. She may realize that she has done something wrong. I hope so. She may simply have gone along with Mr. Ravi, whom she had known for several years. She may not have been able to stand up to him.

Discussion

In the United States, persons are presumed innocent until proven guilty. This is a bedrock principle. I have respected this principle in this article. I have also asserted that taking responsibility for doing something wrong has consequences for the good. I have provided examples and language for what to do and say when we have done something wrong.

We make mistakes. We hurt others. The best course of action is to take responsibility, apologize, and do what it takes not to repeat these hurtful actions. Self-respect and the respect of others result.

Like almost everyone else, Mr. Noah and Mr. Levi have internalized antigay ideologies. In times of stress, Mr. Bryant and

Mr. Levi let go of their common decency and yelled antigay slurs. They can do better. Mr. Noah is trying to live up to his own values.

If what Mr. Levi did is found to be true, then Mr. Levi wanted to have fun. He did. Had he thought about the long-term consequences of his public joke on Mr. Clementi, he may not have done what he did. Mr. Levi thought only of himself. He wanted to bring attention to himself at the expense of others.

Mr. Levi is young. Maybe he will learn that doing harm to others often feels really good. The first step is to realize that your actions are or could be harmful. Mr. Levi did not know this or did not care. So, he did what made him feel good. He probably feels pretty bad now. Taking responsibility for what he is thought to have done may help him feel good again.

Mr. Strauss-Kahn, if he did what the woman said he did, has internalized beliefs about what he is entitled to. Many men throughout the world have a sense of entitlement to sex, especially sex with people others define as their social inferiors. Mr. Strauss-Kahn and others may have learned that they do not have rights to sex with others just because it is what they want. There are laws in countries throughout the world against this. Maybe one day, more sexually entitled people will internalize these laws.

As for Ms. Wei, who pled guilty to invasion of privacy charges, Joseph Clementi, Tyler's father, said a few weeks ago, "Ms. Wei's actions, although unlawful, are substantially different in their nature and extent than the actions of Tyler's former roommate."

Mr. Clementi had more to say about Ms. Wei: "Actions have consequences. We wish that Ms. Wei will become a persons who will make better decisions, will help people and show kindness to those she comes in contact with."

There is no way of knowing, of course, how Ms. Wei will live her life. Let's hope she has learned what she needs to learn to avoid participating in something as hurtful as what has been alleged.

Note: Mr. Ravi was convicted. Mr. Strauss-Kahn was acquitted.

References

Abrams, Johnathan (2011). Noah fined $50,000 for using antigay slur. *New York Times*, May 24, B13, B17.

Gilgun, Jane F. (2010). Evil feels good: Think before you act. *Roots of Violence, Seeds of Change, 1 (2)*. Chapter in present book. http://www.amazon.com/s/ref=nb_sb_noss?url=search-alias%3Daps&field-keywords=Jane+Gilgun+evil+feels+good

Gilgun, Jane F. (2010). *On being a shit: Unkind deeds and cover-ups in everyday life*. Amazon, Kindle, & iBooks, Nook

Molly Wei to testify against Tyler Clementi's roommate Dharun Ravi as part of plea deal. *Star Ledger*, Saturday, May 07, 2011. http://www.nj.com/news/index.ssf/2011/05/molly_wei_defendant_in_tyler_c_1.html

Perez-Pena, Richard & Nate Schweber (2011). Roommate is arraigned in suicide case. *New York Times*, May 24, p. A23.

Rashbaum, William K. (2011). DNA said to link ex-IMF leader and hotel housekeeper. *New York Times*, May 24, p. A21.

21

Fake Accountability & True: Telling the Difference

Telling fake from true accountability can be difficult when the person who is at fault has long experience in covering up their misdeeds. This article discusses three qualities associated with true accountability: Completeness of description, first-person statements, and acceptance of recrimination

When someone apologizes for doing something wrong, how can you tell if they are sincere or faking it? Telling true accountability from fake requires the wit of a Clever Fox. People who fake it give the appearance of accountability, and they often declare their sincere sorrow. Such actions instill hope that they are accountable and will change their ways.

Some enactors learn to fake accountability while young. An example is an older sibling who torments younger siblings when the parents are not present. The younger children complain to parents who make the older child apologize. The apology is duly offered, but as soon as the parents are absent, the older child once again mocks, teases, and harasses the younger children. The apology meant nothing.

Nick is a guy who displayed fake accountability on at least two occasions. Nick had cheated on Cara. He declared himself a bastard and said he had hurt Cara. He then offered to answer any questions Cara had. He kept seeing the other woman, and he answered Cara's questions with jokes, lies, and evasions. He did not follow through on his word. Therefore, **a principle that separates fake accountability from true is whether enactors desist from unkind deeds and cover-ups in the future.**

Completeness of Descriptions

A second principle useful in the test of whether accountability is fake or sincere is the completeness of enactors' descriptions of their unkind deeds and cover-ups. The story of Dick Cheney's incomplete accountability after shooting Harry Whittington is an example. He gave the appearance of contrition and accountability, but neither he nor his spokespersons addressed the initial impression that the spokespersons put out that Harry had broken the rules of hunting and Dick had "done nothing wrong."

The story goes as follows. On a quail hunt, Harry had a spectacular shot: he killed two birds with two shots. The birds hit the ground in back of the hunting party. As Harry went to retrieve them, Dick heard the beating of wings as a covey of quail burst up from the grass behind him. Harry may have flushed them. Dick wheeled around and fired.

Harry was between Dick and the quail. Birdshot hit Harry in the face, neck, arm, and chest. A few days later, a pellet migrated to Harry's heart, and he had a heart attack.

Dick said nothing for days. The day after the shooting, a spokesperson explained what happened and blamed Harry. She said, "This all happened pretty quickly," she said. Harry "did not announce — which would be protocol — 'Hey, it's me, I'm coming up.'" She continued, "He didn't do what he was supposed to do. So when a bird flushed and the vice president swung in to shoot it, Whittington was where the bird was."

Another spokesperson said that Dick "was pleased" that Harry was "doing fine and in good spirits." Another spokesperson said that Dick "felt badly, obviously," and he had not been reckless and had not violated any rules. In fact, Dick had not done "anything he wasn't supposed to do."

After four days of relentless public demand, Dick made his first public statement. He gave an exclusive interview to Brit Hume of Fox News. He said he and no one else pulled the trigger, that it was not Harry's fault, and no one else was to blame. Dick stated that he would never be able to erase from his mind the image of Harry falling. "It was, I'd have to say, one of the worst days of my life, at that moment." He noted that he did not know if he had shot the bird he had aimed for. His concern was for Harry.

He responded to the rumor that the reason for the delay in reporting was because he was drunk and he wanted time for the alcohol to clear from his body. He said he had had one beer at lunch. "Nobody was drinking. Nobody was under the influence."

No Correction

What is striking about Dick's account is what no one said. For instance, neither Dick in his interview with Brit Hume nor any of his spokespersons corrected the impression given during the first few days after the shooting that Harry had broken the rules of hunting and Dick had done nothing wrong.

In actuality, for hunting of any kind, the rules are to see your target before you shoot, to make sure you know where each member of your party is before you shoot, and to never sweep around without knowing who or what is in your line of fire.

In bird hunting, the rule is not to fire until you can see the sky between the earth and the bird and not until the silhouette of the target is against the sky. Further details about the rules of hunting are posted on many websites including that of the Texas Parks and Wildlife Department (TPWD) that publish the Ten Commandments of Shooting Safety. Harry was where he was supposed to be: retrieving the birds he had shot.

Machiavelli: The Rules of Fakery

Machiavelli's advice to politicians comes to mind here. His advice was to follow up unkind acts with the pretense of contrition, which Dick did. He was effusive in his concern for Harry and Harry's family. He conveniently overlooked facts, such as it was he who had violated rules of hunting and Harry had not violated any. He did not speak these simple truths. He let stand the initial impression that Harry had broken the rules of hunting and he had not.

Not correcting the impression that Harry had been at fault is a deception that Machiavelli would have included in his second edition of his book, had he written one.

First-Person Statements

A third principle that separate true accountability from fake is whether enactors state that they are responsible and not some vague group of unnamed individuals. Vagueness gives the appearance of honesty, but is in fact a deflection of responsibility. The phrase "mistakes were made" accomplishes this. U.S. Attorney General Alberto Gonzales uttered this phrase when he attempted to convince the press, the nation, and maybe even other parts of the world that he took responsibility for the firing of eight U.S. attorneys in the fall of 2006.

Had he said, "I made mistakes," then he might have convinced others that he was being accountable. He then explained that he has more than one hundred thousand people under his command and that he delegates many tasks, including the task of firing the attorneys. Someone among the one hundred thousand apparently made a mistake, but not Mr. Gonzales.

"Mistakes were made" is like a mantra among persons who want to save face by faking their way out of having their cover-ups exposed. Paul Wolfowitz insisted that the phrase "mistakes were made all around" be inserted into the documents that described why he left as president of the World Bank in May 2007. His mistake was to approve a huge raise for his life partner who worked for the bank. What appeared in the document was "a number of mistakes were made by a number of individuals." Who made the mistakes, when, and for what purpose are unstated.

Paul further whitewashed his mistakes by making sure that the World Bank statement listed his accomplishments as president. By so doing and by being vague about who was at fault, Paul provided a model of what enactors of unkind deeds and cover-ups can do to save face when they are found out. As John Broder noted in a *New York Times* article, the phrase "mistakes were made" is a "familiar fallback" among politicians.

Broder listed several politicians who used that phrase to weasel out of taking personal responsibility for their behaviors. They included Richard M. Nixon, Ronald Reagan, and Bill Clinton.

Acceptance of Recrimination

Accountable persons listen to and hear what the persons they hurt have to say. This is the fourth principle of accountability. As research on lying shows, backed up by common sense, when liars are found out, recipients are hurt, sad, and full of recrimination. The only way for enactors of unkind deeds and cover-ups to know how their behaviors affected others would be to listen carefully and really hear what others say. It is not easy to face up to hurt and anger that one has caused. The reward is a clear conscience, even if recipients are not ready to carry on with a relationship. In many cases, listening and hearing leads to relationship repair.

Discussion

Four principles guide enactors who want to be accountable for their unkind deeds and cover-ups: no repeats of the bad behavior, completeness of the account, "I" statements, and acceptances of recrimination. Doing so is not easy. For many enactors, becoming accountable requires them to examine and transform beliefs about cowardice and self-respect. Some may believe admitting fault is a sign of weakness. With prideful stubbornness, they refuse to be accountable out of fear of appearing weak.

In actuality, accountable persons recognize that it takes courage to admit wrongdoing. They know they are risking a great deal when they do so. Those who do not see accountability as an act of courage instead resort to cover-up. They miss out on the relief and joy of coming clean and having a clear conscience. For the sake of these beliefs, they are stuck with the smudges and smarminess that go along with lies. They damage their self-respect and lose the respect of others.

Note: This essay is a slightly revised excerpt from *On Being a Shit: Unkind Deeds & Cover-Ups in Everyday Life*, which is available on Amazon, iBooks, Nook, and other booksellers.

22

A Loving Act that Results in Harm: A Review of Sarah's Key, a Film
2011

Sarah's Key *is a French film that raises questions about contrition, self-forgiveness, and redemption after committing an act that results in harm. In the story within the story, Sarah, an 11 year-old girl locked her younger brother Michele in a closet to keep him from being taken when the French rounded up 70,000 Jews in Paris during World War II and brought them to concentration camps. In this article, I wonder whether the harm that resulted from Sarah's actions represent sin and evil. I conclude that when we harm others not only is contrition important, but so are also forgiveness and redemption. Sarah's story is dramatic because she got to the contrition, but not to self-forgiveness. In some ways, her final act may have been redemptive to her but that, too, brought harm.*

I had a conversation with a friend last week after seeing the movie *Sarah's Key*. The movie is a story within a story. The "within" story is about Sarah, who is 11. Sarah locked her younger brother Michele in a closet to keep him from being taken when French authorities rounded up 70,000 Jews in Paris during WW II and brought them to concentration camps. The "within" story involved the consequences of Sarah's act. My friend asked if I thought an act is evil if the person does not intend to harm others. I said, yes, because the act has harmed someone.

Actions That Hurt Others

Later, I realized I had more to say about this. I've been thinking about evil for many years because most of my research has involved interviewing men and some women who have hurt other people to the point where police charged them with felonies and they were in prison. When my friend asked me that question, I had just said I think evil is composed of acts that hurt others.

Within a few days, in a course I am taking on the Old

Testament, the homework was the following question: **What do you think of the idea that we sin even when we do not intend to do so, or are unaware that this has happened?** This was my answer.

This depends on our definition of sin. American pragmatists say that we judge actions by their consequences. For me, sin is harm that I have done to others. If I harm someone without realizing it or without intending to, I have still harmed and therefore I have sinned. The seriousness of the sin depends upon circumstances. If I know my acts are going to harm someone, then that sin is more serious than if I am unaware or the harmful act is not intentional. Unaware/unintentional sin requires a lot of our attention. We must do whatever we can to become more aware of the consequences of our actions so as not to harm others.

I was happy to share this because I rarely have opportunities to say out loud what I am thinking about my research. I sensed that a few people in the Old Testament class had trouble with my point of view, although they didn't say anything. I think this kind of thinking gave my friend pause. He did not respond to me, either, but seemed to be thinking about it.

Ideas of Harming Others

If I were a teacher and saw my class respond this way, I may have figured out a way to elicit responses. I might state my sense that maybe this is something they want to think about. Some may want to dispute it or to investigate whether they understood what I said or intended to say. I might have invited comments during that class and then returned to the topic again in the next class.

With my friend, I will bring up the topic with him again. I will also listen to what others say in order to understand how they understand sin.

Were Sarah's Actions Evil?

As I write this essay, I am wondering if my friend was thinking about Sarah's actions. This gives me pause. Sarah was acting out of love. She wanted to protect her younger brother. She did everything she could to get back to her little brother. When she did.... I don't want to give away the whole story.

Sarah's benevolent intention led to harm. Besides her brother and her parents who were distraught over Sarah's actions, the consequences of her action also harmed herself. There was no one who was able to help her come to terms with the harm her act of love had led to. She had wonderful foster parents, but Sarah apparently was too hurt--she was unable to let go of the hurt she had experienced. About 20 years later, Sarah committed another act that deeply hurt her one child, her son, and her husband, both of whom apparently forgave her.

So, there it is. Sarah did two major actions that led to profound hurt. Her actions that led to hurt had understandable motivations. One motivation was her love of her brother and her desire to protect him. This action has mitigating circumstances. Sarah was about 11 years old, when her executive skills--her thinking skills--were not fully developed. She could not foresee that she might not be able to get back to her brother soon, although she thought she would be back that night, and that he would not be able to get out of the closet because she had locked him in.

When she committed an act that hurt her son and husband, she may have been unable to work through her own guilt and get to the hurt she would cause them. This, too, means she may not have had good executive skills in this situation. If she thought about the harm and did the harmful act anyway, then this points to the power of her own guilt about her brother and the effects of her actions on her parents.

I feel presumptuous in saying that Sarah's acts are evil or were sins. If I stick with my definition of sin and evil, I would have to say yes.

Contrition, Forgiveness, & Redemption

The mitigating circumstances are such that the necessity of forgiveness and redemption becomes clear. The story of Sarah is more dramatic when she does not find forgiveness, redemption, and resurrection. She clearly took responsibility for her actions and did feel contrition.

For the rest of though, for us to live loving lives, we have to go through the whole process. Otherwise, we will feel guilt, unworthiness, and self-hatred, which separates us from others and ourselves and can spiral to the point where we are bitter and angry, although undoubtedly we still have moments of peace and grace.

Sarah's Key is a wonderful story that kept my attention and led to writing this essay.

Part 4: The Prevention of Violent Behaviors

23

How to Teach Children to be Violent Offenders

This article begins with what parents can do to teach children to become sex offenders. There are only a few simple steps. A lot of people do it. You can, too. Please note that this is satire. This purpose of the article actually is inform parents, professionals, and a concerned public about how to prevent children from becoming sex offenders. This is not satire. Prevention is hard. People must really want to do it. Apparently, not enough of us do. As a result, we keep on raising hundreds of thousands of children a year to become sex offenders. Is that what we want.

It's easy to teach children to become violent. First, teach them that using others for their own gain in the way to go. What matters is what they want. What others want does not matter. You could go that extra distance and teach them that they should hurt others if others do them wrong. Vengeance is important in teaching children how to certain kinds of violent offenders. That's the kind that enjoys believes two wrongs might a right. Making others suffer provides deep satisfaction when vengeance is a motive. Other kinds of sex offenders talk themselves into believing that they are being violent for the victims' own good. These sex offenders have some ethics!

Second, avoid talking about sex with your children or make sure you have loads of sexual material, sexual talk, and sexual activity in your family home. Quite effective. It's super effective if you do both.

Three, make sure you teach your children not to talk about things that bother them. Shame them if necessary. Tell them in many different ways how proud you are of them that they've got guts because they don't show emotions like fear, sadness, or shame. Sometimes you don't have to say a thing. Just act that way yourself. Your kids will pick up on how to behave.

Four, make sure your children feel unsafe in your family. Be too busy with your own affairs to find out what they are doing, what interests them, and what bothers them. Better yet, yell at them, beat them, and call them names. You could do one or more of these things. It doesn't really matter. The important thing is to make sure they feel unimportant, like a little black dot that no one notices. This contradicts number 1, but sex offenders are full of contradictions.

Five, if your children have experienced traumas, such the death of a parent, repeated changes of caregivers, child sexual abuse, and witnessing violence, be sure to say the child needs to put all of this in the past. And stick to it. Avoid professional help at all costs. If you want to be extra sure that your children become violent offenders, here are a few other things you can do. Discourage them for talking to anyone about their trauma. Punish them if they do.

Six, make your children think you think they are the best children in the world, kind and decent and incapable of being less than paragons of virtue. If something bad happens to them, you can be sure they will not tell you because then you will think they are not perfect. So, raise perfectionists and be perfect yourself. Don't worry if this guideline contradicts the others. You can make your children feel unsafe, discourage them from talking about their difficult experiences, and tell them they are the best children in the world, all at once. It works!

Seven, if other people blame your children for something, protect them at all costs. Go on the offensive. Make sure that other people know that everyone else is at fault, but not your children and certainly not you. Make sure your children never learn to be accountable. Above all, make sure you show them that accountability is for cowards. Never, never apologize. Apologies are for weaklings. Keep on making them feel unsafe and do all the other things that this article recommends.

Eight, protect your own image no matter what. If other people say your children have done something wrong, accuse them of bias—any kind of bias. Racial, religious, gender, and income level are great ways to disable anyone who criticizes you.

Just follow these steps. They practically guarantee that your child will be a violent offender, unless your children have the misfortune to find other people who will coddle them and actually encourage them to go against all that you have taught them. Keep your children away from kind, loving people at all costs. These people will promote their own agendas and persuade your children to talk about things that bother them and will help your children to realize that negotiating for what you want is rewarding. You don't want your kids to grow up weak, emotional, and imperfect.

If social policy helps you raise violent offenders, all the better. Pat's story is an example of what you can hope for. Pat came from a small town where his family had lived for generations. His parents did all they could to ensure that he become a sex offender. They followed all of the above steps. They even had help from the school principal. Pat, a third grader, told the principal that his mother beats him. The principal did not believe Pat. He phoned Pat's mother to tell her what Pat had said.

The principal had known Pat's mother all his life. He knew the mother would never beat Pat. When Pat got home, his mother beat him for talking to the principal. Pat never again looked to other people to help him. Instead, he made himself feel better by spying on his older brothers having sex with girlfriends. He masturbated to the soft porn that was in the home. Masturbation made him feel better, too. At 13, he was in juvenile detention for sexually assaulting a 12 year-old girl.

These steps really do work. The next essay in this book is about the prevention of violent behaviors.

24

The Prevention of Sexually Abusive Behaviors

This article focuses on child sexual abuse, but the points I make apply well to the prevention of other forms of violence as well.

Prevention includes preventing the development of sexually abusive behaviors in the first place. Sexual abusers were children once. They are not born as sexual abusers. They learn to abuse children sexually. This learning begins in childhood. They learn that sexual behaviors with children feel good, lift their mood, or make them feel loved. They do not care what the children want. They learn to be self-centered and self-absorbed. They have poor executive skills. They learn to be emotionally detached from others. They learn the beliefs that lead them to abuse children.

Most U.S.-based child sexual abuse prevention programs teach children how to avoid being sexually abused. As important as children's self-protection is, this places far too much responsibility on children, allows adults not to take responsibility for protecting children, and ignores those who truly are responsible: perpetrators. The focus of prevention must be on the prevention of sexually abusive behaviors in the first place. Child sexual abuse is preventable. Adults have the responsibility for prevention.

A Foundation for Prevention

The information in this book provides a foundation for the prevention of child sexual abuse. As has been shown, sensitive, responsive parents socialize their children to be sensitive and responsive young people and adults who engage in sensitive, responsive relationships with others. Individuals raised this way choose sexual partners who are generational equals and with whom they engage in reciprocal, affirming, and egalitarian relationships. They are sensitive and responsive to children. This rules out engaging children in sexual contact and rules in recognizing children's vulnerabilities. This also rules in the need for protected environments where children can thrive without demands that are beyond their capacities developmentally.

This book also has shown that most children with risks for becoming sexual abusers of children do not. They have the personal and social resources to cope with, adapt to, and overcome the risks and adversities that might make them capable of sexually abuse children. Most survivors are resilient, but they become resilient because people around them are sensitive and responsive.

Emotional Expressiveness

The chief factor that appears to protect children from becoming perpetrators of child sexual abuse is emotional expressiveness, which is defined at length in chapter eleven and illustrated in several other chapters. When children, adolescents, and adults have capacities for emotional expressiveness, this means they

- have experienced sensitive, responsive, and contingently reciprocal relationships with other people over time, typically with their parents and also with others;

- can experience, identify, and express appropriately a range of feelings;

- understand and identify with (empathize with) the emotions of others;

- encourage the healthy emotional expression of others; and

- have good executive skills as shown by their flexible thinking and problem-solving abilities that includes capacities for considering alternative and for thinking through consequences of their actions.

When individuals have capacities for emotional expressiveness, histories of secure attachments, and good executive skills, they realize that acting without considering the effects on others may hurt others and is unfair. When they are stressed, anxious, and angry, they engage their executive skills and seek pro-social ways of coping, such as talking to others, considering alternative actions and the consequences of these actions, and any number of other strategies discussed in this book. They do not use children to "fix" how they feel, as do many perpetrators of child sexual abuse. In short, they re-regulate in pro-social ways. They resist pro-violence influences to which they have been exposed because they have the emotional resources and executive skills to do so.

Some perpetrators do not abuse children as a means to re-regulate. These abusers abuse simply because abuse makes them feel good. Such abusers have obvious deficits in their emotional development and executive skills. They are unable to understand and empathize with the emotions and rights of others. They do not have the executive skills to see the harm they inflict when they use children sexually. What they want over-rides any consideration of effects on children. They absorb pro-violence beliefs because they do not have the emotional resources and executive skills necessary to see how harmful these beliefs are.

Many perpetrators provide vivid portraits of their parents as emotionally insensitive and non-responsive. Skip did this as reported earlier in this book. It is not difficult to imagine how Skip developed the emotional insensitivity, self-centeredness, and lack of executive skills that led to his abuse of Aria and other children. Unlike Skip, other perpetrators may have had "good enough" parents, but they still abuse children. John's and Cyrus's cases are examples.

Some perpetrators, however, are unable to provide researchers and practitioners with the fine details of the relationships with parents and others. This is the case for the story Mike told. He painted broad brush strokes in terms of his parents' and siblings' adequacy, such as spending time with him, going to church with him, and visiting him in prison, but he did not tell any stories that showed they abused or neglected him or were otherwise insensitive and non-responsive.

Whether they held him accountable for the abuse is not known. One sister apparently did, by refusing to visit him in prison. In fact, it is unknown whether his parents held him accountable for misbehaviors and transgressions of rules as he was growing up. His extreme insensitivity to his wife and stepdaughter suggests that he had a stunted sense of accountability that could be linked to his parents' lax enforcement of the rules of proper conduct. Mike's parents may have been permissive with him, and not authoritative. Authoritative parents combine unconditional love, clear rules, simple rewards for following rules, and appropriate penalties for breaking rules. Mike may not have had these advantages.

Since some perpetrators are unable to provide the details needed to draw direct conclusions and because they show an incredible insensitivity and lack of responsiveness themselves, the logical conclusion is that they did not experience their parents as sensitive and responsive and did not as a result develop these capacities themselves. This does not mean that their parents had no capacities for emotional responsiveness. It does mean that some perpetrators as children were unable to respond to whatever parents and others were able to offer them that might have helped them to develop emotionally and to develop good executive skills.

Gender

In general, boys are at a disadvantage as compared to girls in their opportunities for optimal emotional development and for the acquisition of good executive skills in interpersonal relationships. Gender has a role to play in understanding and preventing child sexual abuse. Boys and men perpetrate up to 90% of all sexual abuse. Boys and men are taught to be strong and to be forthright and even aggressive about pursuing what they want. They are socialized to be silent and even ashamed of emotions that might suggest vulnerability. They learn that others may call them "sissies," "girls," "fems," "punks," and "gays" if they show sadness, shame, hurt feelings, need for comfort, and fear.

Dogs and horses are like that, too. They hide their vulnerabilities because vulnerabilities endanger the pack or the herd by attracting predators. Hiding vulnerability may be related to a "warrior" mentality, where men have to be strong at all times to fulfill their roles as conquerors, protectors, and procurers of bounty. If they fail in these roles, they risk swift and harsh consequences.

Because of gender-based socialization, boys are less likely than girls to seek others out to work through their fears, worries, and vulnerabilities. Over time, they become inept at handling these emotions constructively and also risk not to develop their executive skills to think through how to cope with, adapt to, and overcome strong emotions. Some, like Mike, distance themselves from their emotions and may even cease to feel them.

As a result, they find it difficult if not impossible to identify with and be compassionate toward the emotions of others and to be concerned with how their sexual abuse affects children. Mike showed no compassion, for example, for his stepdaughter June and for his wife whom he raped "all the time." Many perpetrators show this profound emotional insensitivity and lack of imagination associated with stunted executive skills.

Violence and Discounting Others

Violence, which involves actions that hurt others and that benefit perpetrators, stands for a class of behaviors that over-value one's own interest and discount the worth, wishes, rights, and autonomy of others. In everyday life, children routinely witness physical violence as well as other actions that discount others. Violence and discounting comes to them in many forms, through advertisements, comic books, television shows, toys, the Internet, and video and computer games. The violence may be sexual as well as physical. Men of action perpetrate violence against "weaker" men and women. These media glamorize violence and show its rewards.

Children who grow up in safe, sensitive, and responsive families and communities are exposed to these influences, as are children who grow up in families and communities where violence is routine and an everyday occurrence. These children learn that various types of violence offer survival, status, material rewards, and self-enhancement.

Children who have secure attachments have opportunities to process the violent and other discounting behaviors they witness. They learn from direct instruction not to hurt others. Parents and others model and teach appropriate ways of expressing themselves and getting what they want. Their parents and others are there for them to show them that violence hurts other people. Such children are at relatively low risk to internalize the pro-violence beliefs and actions to which they are exposed.

The lessons of violence do not become part of their inner working models of themselves, others, and how the world works. These individuals grow into adults who say "The thought never crossed my mind" when asked why they have never sexually abused children. They say the same thing when asked about rape. Some may admit that they sometimes say such words as, "I am so angry I could kill him or her." They sometimes have violent thoughts and emotions. They do not act on these thoughts and emotions because they have automatic protective responses that help them to realize that such actions hurt others and themselves.

However, if children's inner landscape matches the outer landscape of the violence and discounting to which they are exposed, children are more likely to believe that violence and discounting are not only permissible but obligatory if they are to have self respect and are to protect themselves. Since violence is heavily gendered, boys are more likely to identify with aggressors and believe they should be aggressive themselves. Entitlement to take what they want becomes part of their inner working models. If they discover that sex with children feels good to them, they take what they want.

Sexualized Children

Children who have been sexualized through sexual abuse or exposure to sexualized environments require special care. Sensitive, responsive adults must ensure that child survivors receive professional help in order to work through the effects of being sexually abused. Some perpetrators like Cyrus, discussed in chapter thirteen, become sexualized at young ages. They act out with other children as young children. They perpetrate against children in various ways throughout their lives. Had Cyrus's sexual abuse come to light at the time it happened, he would not have been a life-long abuser. His life trajectory would have been like John's, whose case is reported in chapter twelve. Cyrus's parents were "good enough" and would have been there for him as John's has been for John.

At the other end of a continuum are children like Chuck, who was sexualized through sexual abuse while a preschooler and had such a risk pile-up, including neurological issues, that the only way public authorities knew to keep him and children around him safe was to place him in residential treatment. He may have been able to stay in the community had his mother undergone therapy for her own history of abuse. She did not.

Chuck's mother, therefore, was unable to provide him with the stable, predictable, and safe environment he required; in fact, her lifestyle exposed him to the multiple risks that led to his serious behavioral problems. Chuck may have been a difficult child to raise because of possible neurological issues, but the long-term and multiple risks to which his mother's lifestyle exposed him were highly detrimental and may have contributed to his neurological issues. By his absence, Chuck's biological father contributed to Chuck's issues.

Many children in the United States have histories similar to Chuck's. Some children with multiple risks do not have neurological issues. This is an advantage because it is one less adversity with which children and their families must deal. If their parents work through their own histories of trauma and become sensitive and responsive, there is hope that the children can work through the effects of multiple risks and do not become sexual abusers for their lifetimes.

If parents refuse to deal with their own histories of trauma and are unable to protect their children from many other adversities that become risk factors for sexually acting out, then children are on their way to being life-long sexual abusers, as was the case for Chuck and is the case for many other children.

In some cases, child protection local authorities step in and bring cases to court when concerns are high for children's well-being. Social service agencies may recommend foster care and adoption, and the courts may agree. In such cases, there is hope that foster and adoptive parents can provide the safety, structure, and love that children require in order to learn to cope with, adapt to, and overcome multiple risks associated with sexually abusing children and other destructive outcomes.

Prevention

Everyone has a part to play in prevention. Our social system is complex. Our responses, therefore, have to be on many different levels that reflect not only the complexity of our social organization but also the complexity of the influences that lead to the sexual abuse of children. Prevention of child sexual abuse requires actions on the individual, familial, community, statewide, countrywide, and international levels. Anything individuals or groups do to promote children's well-being contributes to prevention. Something as small as a kind word to a child or as long-term as advocating for policy and program changes contribute to prevention.

Universal Prevention

The information in this book provides a foundation for many different kinds of social actions that can contribute to the prevention of the sexual abuse of children. Some policies and programs are already providing such services, often, however, without realizing how important the programs are to child sexual abuse prevention. To be more mindful that emotional expressiveness, healthy sex educations, executive skills, and awareness of how respect and empathy contribute to child sexual abuse prevention can make these programs more effective and responsive. Such programs are example of universal or primary preventions strategies, or strategies that are aimed at the general population. Unfortunately, such programs do not exist in sufficient numbers to meet the need.

Selective Prevention

Selective prevention efforts target at-risk individuals, meaning individuals whose life circumstances and beliefs could lead to adverse outcomes or already have. *Secondary* and *tertiary prevention* are terms used to describe types of selective prevention. Secondary prevention involves policies and programs designed to promote optimal development in individuals at risk for poor outcomes. Tertiary prevention involves policies and programs for persons how already have poor outcomes.

Examples of secondary prevention are parent education groups and other psychoeducation programs where individuals receive information and skills training that help them to cope with, adapt to, and overcome the effects of their own experiences of abuse and neglect. When parents and others participate successfully in these programs, they become more emotionally expressive and less self-absorbed and therefore more sensitively responsive to their own children, to their life partners, and to other people in general. They also learn strategies for dealing with the many challenges involved in raising children.

Tertiary prevention involves interventions for individuals, children, teens, adults and their families, where a condition has already appeared, such as sexually abusive behaviors. Examples are treatment programs for children and their families where the children have been sexually abused or who experienced other adversities. These programs are described in some detail in chapter twelve. Incapacitation involves removing individuals from society and keeping them confined. Prison and civil commitment are examples of tertiary prevention that involves incapacitation.

Individualization

While there are themes that cross over into different types of prevention efforts, individualization is another principle associated with successful secondary and tertiary prevention programs. One size does not fit all. When crafting and implementing programs and interventions, professionals who are flexible and who tailor what they offer have good chances for success. For example, the principle that emotionally sensitive and responsive parents raise children who are sensitive and responsive is generally true, but there are exceptions.

Rob's parents were insensitive and abusive, but he found other resources on which to build a non-abusive life. Cyrus's parents were probably sensitive and responsive, but he was unable, because of societal taboos that played out in his family, to share his issues with sexual abuse with his parents. Mike presented no evidence that his parents were other than sensitive and responsive.

Typically, effective treatment programs explore clients' capacities for emotional expressiveness, sensitivity to others, executive skills, beliefs about entitlements and taking what you want, and capacities to deal constructively with stress and trauma. In other words, they explore gender-based beliefs, such as men as heads of households who have absolute control over wives and children. Dealing with selfishness and self-centeredness is part of effective treatment programs.

Effective treatment professionals, however, are open-minded enough not to make assumptions about the families of perpetrators, nor about the experiences and beliefs that perpetrators have that might contribute to their sexually abusive behaviors. Professionals must do individualized assessments and be prepared to devise strategies meant to increase the capacities that research and professional experience have identified as factors in the sexual abuse of children. Sensitive responsiveness is the centerpiece of treatment goals, but how professionals nurture sensitive responsiveness in clients requires sensitive responsiveness on their part.

Society's Executive Skills

As a society, we lack good executive skills. We do not see how accepted beliefs and practices result in the sexual abuse of children. Parents and professionals alone cannot change the forces that lead to sexual abuse, although they do what they can to counter these forces within their immediate spheres of influence. Society-wide efforts are required for prevention.

Several issues must be handled well to ensure that children do not sexually abuse others. This includes the sex education of children, encouraging the emotional expression of boys, and challenging beliefs and practices that lead to the sexual abuse of children. The mass media, government, higher education, and religious institutions can make major contributions to child sexual abuse prevention.

The Four Cornerstones of Prevention

Healthy sex education is one of four cornerstones of child sexual abuse prevention. Most parents require a great deal of encouragement and education to talk to their children about sexuality and sexual abuse. Local, national, and international governments, foundations, school boards, religious institutions, and advocacy groups could develop public awareness campaigns to promote healthy sex education in families and in schools and to make educational materials widely available. Through the Internet, these groups could make videos, podcasts, and other materials available to anyone who wants them.

Sex education is still controversial for some, but it is time to pay attention to research and experience that shows that healthy sex education promotes healthy sexual behaviors and reduces unwanted consequences of irresponsible and uninformed sexual behaviors, such as sexual harassment, child sexual abuse, rape, unwanted pregnancies and sex-related diseases.

The second cornerstone is the promotion of emotional expressiveness in boys. Healthy emotional development automatically leads to the acquisitions of good executive skills. This alone would go a long way toward helping children overcome a major risk for abusing others. There could be a massive effort to support sensitive, responsive parenting. Many parents are already, but all parents and their children benefit when there are widely available resources for parents that help them to maintain their sensitive responsiveness.

This is an up-hill battle because of the many sources of distorted depictions of masculinity and femininity, the rewards for meeting gendered expectations, and the punishments for failing to do so. Many gendered expectations interfere with the development of emotional availability and sensitivity.

As discussed earlier, there are many barriers to boys' emotion expressions and many rewards from them to be aggressive and to take what they want. Direct discussion of pro-violence beliefs and alternatives to these beliefs are part of emotion education. Many of the words that punish boys for not conforming to gender expectations, such as "sissies," "fem," and "girls" are sexist; meaning what it means to be male is defined as not being female. Being female is stigmatized. Such gendered strategies of social control are destructive.

A third cornerstone is to devise strategies to encourage and support parents who have experienced trauma to deal with trauma's effects. The other cornerstones—promotion of emotional expressiveness and executive skills and wide-spread sex education—could loosen the rigid resistance that many parents have to dealing with their own issues. Traumatized parents were traumatized children once. Those who refuse to deal with their traumas likely received punitive responses when they tried to talk about their traumas, as did Skip and Monty.

A fourth cornerstone is parent education programs, which, as mentioned, are already available. They can, however, be promoted more widely and many more can be created. In these programs, parents can learn to become more sensitive and responsive than they might have been otherwise. Well-prepared parents raise children who have capacities associated with the formation of intimate relationships with generational equals and who understand and protect vulnerability in themselves and others.

Parents, professionals, and socially aware citizens have important roles to play in promoting universal and selective prevention programs. They can join task forces and citizen groups, work for candidates who understand what children and families need to thrive, research social issues, and lobby local, statewide, national, and international governments. Blogs, letters to editors, and posting advocacy pieces on the Internet are possibilities. Volunteer work at schools, childcare centers, and social service agencies are other ways of contributing to healthy children, families, and societies. We have complex social systems. Effective change will happen when multiple parts of systems change.

Social Skills

Social skills training is a prevention strategy that many adults can implement. Social skills training can help children develop empathy and executive skills. Parents, educators, and others who spend time with children can adapt these approaches to a variety of situations in families, classrooms, and other settings. They can be used as universal prevention strategies or selective.

Children learn social skills through direct instruction and through observing how others behave. They repeat the behaviors that bring them rewards and behaviors that they see are rewarded. The following are examples of guidelines for teaching children social skills. Parents and teachers may want to provide additional guidelines.

Expectations

Children need to know what parents and teachers expect from them. It is important for parents and teachers to set ground rules. Keep them simple. Here are some examples.

Family Etiquette

- No hitting, yelling, pushing, or biting. If someone bothers you, tell him or her to stop.

- If other children continue to bother you, tell me. It's my job to take care of things like that.

- If you bother another child, you will have a time out.

- Give other people a chance to finish talking before you talk.

- Do not use other people's stuff without their permission.

- If you have questions about differences between boys and girls, ask me. Do not inspect the bodies of others, especially of children younger than you.

Classroom Etiquette

- Raise your hand if you want to talk in the classroom.

- Do not interrupt when other children are talking.

- Do not interrupt when I am speaking.

- Stay in your seats until I give you permission to get up.

- Do not push, grab, or shove other children.

- If someone bothers you, tell him or her to stop.

- If someone bothers you and will not stop when you tell them to, tell me. I will take care of it.

- If you bother another child, you will have a time out.

When children follow the rules, recognize them for it. Here are some examples.

- "Thank you, Marcus, for raising your hand when you wanted to speak."

- "Good job, Kylie. Ronald pulled your hair. You told him to stop and that it hurt. He didn't stop. You told me."

- "I can see you really wanted to say something, Jamal. Good for you that you waited until Jordan finished what she had to say."

- "I'm glad you asked. I'm happy to talk to you about kissing boys."

In short, when children perform well in classrooms and at home, it is important to praise them immediately. Rewards increase the chances that children will repeat the behaviors.

Direct Instruction

Something as brief as 10-minute sessions of direct instruction once a week or as needed could have life-long benefits for children. Instruction can create a safe and enjoyable classroom experience and family life. The following are some topics to consider.

- How to ask someone for something.

- How to say "no" to someone who asks you for something.

- How to accept a "no" from someone else.

- How to thank someone who does something nice for you.

- How to disagree with someone.

- How to think about consequences of your actions: Who will they affect? How will they affect them? How will they affect you?

- How to introduce people to each other.

- How to joke with others without hurting them.

- How to apologize.

- How to admit you did something wrong.

- How to make up for doing something wrong.

- How to accept an apology.

- How to help another child when someone is hurting him or her.

- How to ask someone to stop doing something that hurts or bothers you.

- How to ask someone for help when someone is hurting or bothering you.

- How to listen to a friend who is feeling sad.

To teach these skills, first describe the topic. Then provide a brief description of how to respond. Then role play in front of the children how to respond. Next, have the children role play with each other. Have the children play both roles. Praise them when they role play well. Help them problem-solve how to do better if they have difficulties in the role plays. Finally, give the children a few minutes to talk about the activity with each other and with whoever provides the instruction.

During these discussions, teachers have the opportunity to explore children's expectations about gendered-based behaviors and entitlements. They can broaden the discussion to ask children to describe the kinds of interactions they observe in video games, on the Internet, and in movies.

Direct instruction and discussion of these topics contain implicit and explicit messages about emotional expressiveness, boundaries, respect, and empathy. They are counter messages to beliefs about entitlement and taking what you want regardless of what others want.

Teach by Example

How parents and teachers deal with children teaches them a great deal about social skills. When what you do makes them feel good, they are likely to imitate you. When they see that you reward the behaviors you want, children will want those rewards for themselves. Practice good social skills yourself, and the children will learn from you.

In summary, children learn social skills from direct instruction and from observation. Parents and educators are positioned to teach children skills that they will use for the rest of their lives. In the short term, children with good social skills contribute to enjoyable and safe families and classrooms. Social skills training such as those just described can help children develop good executive skills and emotional expressiveness.

Teaching these skills is part of sensitive, responsive parenting and teaching. These skills, in combination with a good sex education, sensitive care of children who have experienced trauma, and countering abuse-supportive beliefs with pro-social beliefs, go a long way toward prevention. Preventing children from becoming sexual abusers is an important goal in prevention programs.

Teaching Moments

In everyday interactions with children, adults have opportunities to promote emotional expressiveness and executive skills. Children can sometimes be rude, impolite, and aggressive toward other children and adults. When this happens, parents and other adults will be most helpful if they have balanced reactions. Over-reacting or dismissing the significance of the behaviors are common, but what counts is for adults to engage their own executive skills and to keep their cool. Such child behaviors are teaching moments.

Adults are helpful when they ask the child to stop the behavior and name the feeling they think the child is experiencing. Often that is enough. Naming a feeling for a child often calms the child because the child feels understood. In calm states of mind, parents and educators can engage their own executive skills and talk with children about how they can handle their emotions more effectively the next time.

Children are eager to have friends and to belong. To do so, they have to learn how to get along with others. Teaching children how to respectfully express what they want and do not want or what they like or do not like can lead children to build healthy relationships. Respect means that children take into consideration what others want, they know how to negotiate so as to find common ground, and they know not to take advantage of others to get what they want.

Remind children of the rules. Gently guide them to time out if you have set time out as the consequence for such behaviors. Keep the time out brief. Even a minute or two can be long enough. The following guidelines can help in difficult situations with children.

- Remind children that all feelings are okay, but they do need to think about how they express their feelings. Expressing themselves with rudeness and disrespect, with verbal aggression, verbal abuse, excluding or ignoring, physical aggression, or sexual aggression are not okay. Telling someone to back off or saying, "I don't like how you're behaving," or "Don't speak to me that way," or "I find your behaviors hurtful" are direct and clear expressions of feelings that do no harm. They are okay.

- Attend to the child who has been hurt. Children who are rude and impolite hurt others. Children who have been hurt gain in self-confidence and self-respect when others comfort them and help them to figure out how to stand up for themselves while also not harming others themselves.

Another variation on acting without thinking is when children and adults, for that matter, "go for the jugular;" that is, act without thinking when someone does something they do not like. They immediately become angry and engage "low road" responses that can involve thinking angry thoughts, name calling, and hitting and kicking. For some, sexual aggression can result, or sexualized self-soothing. Fortunately, children—and adults—typically can restrain themselves, but they also have no idea how to engage their "high road" responses and thus to negotiate with others to find common ground. They therefore silence themselves. This undermines connection and relationships.

For children to be able to handle such situations, they have to see that people around them have effective strategies for doing so. They also require direct instruction. The instruction would include 1) noticing that they are about to act without thinking, 2) consider what they really want, 3) and think about the various ways that they can get what they want and also maintain a healthy connection with others.

Guidelines that can help in such situations include 1) being clear about what they want, 2) telling other people what they want, 3) listening to others in order to understand what they want, and 4) engaging in a search for ways to accommodate each other. Sometimes what we want is unacceptable or not possible. In those situations, children need to develop capacities to accept such possibilities, but they have the right to know the reasons why certain things cannot happen. Children eventually internalize parental guidelines and direct instruction. They become skilled in handing conflict situations. They also know that they can go to their parents and other adults if they need some help.

Teach Alternative Behaviors

Children may sometimes need direct instruction about their behaviors when they do not realize that their behaviors hurt others. It is important that parents make it clear that some behaviors are not allowed. The next step is to teach behaviors that are allowed to replace them. For example, you could say to a child, "When you do that, it hurts other people." Problem-solving is helpful. How else could they tell others what they want? Children often respond well to examples.

Parents and teachers can have a big impact in seemly small events. Janie, five, yelled at Sylvia, also five, "You're a liar" during play time in kindergarten. Sylvia was indeed lying. However, the kindergarten teacher was so concerned about Janie's rudeness that she gave Janie a time out and told her to sit in the corner behind the grand piano. Janie cried and felt ashamed. The teacher missed an opportunity to teach Janie new social skills. She could have told Janie, "Speaking so loudly and calling someone a liar hurts. If you don't agree with Sylvia, you can say, 'I don't agree.' Instead of providing guidance, the teacher's actions provoked shame and hurt in this young child.

Few children at five have the skills and awareness to respond firmly but empathically to someone whose behaviors concern them. After the teacher's reprimand, Janie still did not know how to express concerns about others' behaviors, but the next time she wanted to disagree she would remember her prior punishment. She would then be at risk to yell ever louder, be even more rude, or to say nothing and seethe. She might even feel guilty and at fault for objecting to another's poor behaviors.

Sylvia, of course, needed some attention and instruction as well. The teacher could have acknowledged that Sylvia might have been hurt by Janie's words, and she could have told Sylvia that when you say something that another child does not believe, the child may challenge you. The teacher might not have known whether Sylvia was lying or not, but she could have helped Sylvia understand that other people may disagree with her but they have no right to be rude and aggressive.

Eventually, the teacher could have worked out a way to repair the children's relationship. When both children had settled down, understood what went wrong, and felt safe, the teacher could have encouraged Janie to apologize for her aggression and also state she disagreed with Sylvia. Sylvia could have admitted she did not tell the truth and would do better the next time. She could have accepted Janie's apology.

This kind of guidance takes teacher time and skill but it is important to do. Children sometimes mistake verbal aggression for humor. Something as simple as helping children understand that words hurt may help children realize that they have to stop doing something.

Final Words

Child sexual abuse is a serious social problem that undermines the well-being and life chances of millions of children in the United States and world-wide. Accurate understanding of sexual abuse, sensitive responsiveness to children, and direct instruction about emotion expression, respectful behaviors, and sexuality are steps toward creating a societies where child sexual abuse is rare or non-existent.

Child sexual is a complex social problem that few people understand well. Myths and misunderstandings lead many to believe that they do understand. What child and adult survivors, perpetrators, and mothers say about child sexual abuse adds important dimensions to knowledge and provides a basis for policy, prevention, and intervention. Perpetrators take advantage of children. It is that simple. Perpetrators are selfish. It is that simple. Children require sensitive, responsive care. It is that simple.

Prevention is more complex. Many influences come together when individuals perpetrate child sexual abuse. Some of these influences have strong social support, such as the pairing of masculinity and aggression, especially sexual aggression, the pairing of masculinity and suppression of feelings, and the sense of entitlement that some have to take what they want. Self-gratification and callous disregard for the well-being of children characterize perpetrators of child sexual abuse.

While cattle instinctively form protective circles around unrelated young to ward off danger, human beings allow child sexual abuse to continue. Our social systems are more complicated than that of cattle, but our executive skills are superior to those of cattle. When it comes to child sexual abuse, however, our executive skills are poor, with some exceptions. We have extreme reactions to perpetrators whom we can identify, typically strangers who abuse children. We spent huge sums of money for prisons and civil commitment, while we provide woefully inadequate services for child survivors and their families. Furthermore, we do not have the executive skills to connect the dots that might prevent the development of sexually abusive behaviors in the first place.

The promotion of boys' emotional development, large-scale commitment of resources to promote healthy sex education, challenges to gender role socialization that put boys at risk to perpetrate, parent education and training, and enlightened efforts to help traumatized parents deal with their own trauma are some of the many strategies that will contribute to primary prevention. This book has discussed and documented these strategies.

Efforts at every level of our society are required. Advocacy through task forces and citizens' groups, policy changes and resources to implement and monitor programs, training programs for professionals based on accurate, multi-faceted information, and many other efforts already discussed in this book are some of the many ways to make a difference. Volunteer work with children and their families in homeless shelters and children's homes, guardian ad litem programs, and reading to children in school are some of the many ways that individuals can make a difference in individual children's lives.

The roots of child sexual abuse are wide-spread and are connected to many other social ills. Almost any effort that promotes child and parent well-being contributes to prevention. Parent support programs, for, example, have positive effects that include and go beyond the prevention of child sexual abuse. There simply are not enough of them. Healthy and appropriate sex education, emotion and social skills education in the schools, and programs that challenge pro-violence beliefs are other interventions that contribute to prevention.

Children who have secure attachments to their parents are much more likely to receive healthy sex educations and to be raised by parents who practice gender egalitarianism. It would never occur to them to take advantage of others. If, as young children, they do attempt to do so, their parents immediately correct them and show them how to behave in respectful ways.

While this is wonderful, there are countless millions of children already at risk because of insecure and disorganized attachments and who receive their sex education and guidance for sexual behaviors from uninformed peers and the media that presents exploitive images of sexual behaviors in order to turn a profit. Such children have complex risks for various poor outcomes. Some of them perpetrate child sexual abuse. An educated public with good executive skills would take immediate action to provide children and families with the resources they require to thrive. There is much to be done.

Neglected Social Problem

Child sexual abuse affects the quality of life of hundreds of millions of people in the United States and world-wide. Few conditions affect that many people. Yet, aside from huge media reaction and legislation meant to incapacitate perpetrators, child sexual abuse is one of the most neglected social problems in modern times. Survivors often have no one to talk to and families are on their own to figure out what to do. The public discourses focuses on perpetrators, with the result that services and care for child survivors are inadequate.

Few services exist in the United States and internationally. The general public remains uneducated. What they know is informed by myths and misunderstandings with the result that most children believe sexual abuse is their own fault. Most survivors suffer in silence out of fear of the responses they will get if they talk about it. In many countries, victims are ostracized and even killed. Family members protect perpetrators and punish victims out of fear of public disgrace and destitution. When peers learn that a child has been sexually abused, some bully and harass child survivors to the point where children have to transfer schools to maintain any semblance of mental health.

The lack of public will to provide services and wide-spread education protects perpetrators. As a result, child sexual abuse continues. I have been working in the field for almost thirty years and continue to hope that one day there will be a world-wide awakening to what we are allowing to happen to so many children.

Note: This is the last chapter of the book *Child Sexual Abuse: From Harsh Realities to Hope,* available for e-readers and as a paperback original on Amazon.

25

Three Principles for the Prevention of Sexually Abusive Behaviors and Sexual Assault

This article offers three general ideas associated with the prevention of sexually harmful behaviors. They are relationships with others, capacities for negotiations, and appreciation of the sweetness of sex. An agreed upon understanding is like a road map that These simple ideas cover many complex underlying issues. Whatever kinds of prevention programs that various groups of people develop, effective programs will incorporate these three ideas in their own individualized ways.

I interviewed perpetrators of child sexual abuse, rape, and other forms of violence for more than 25 years. I did this because I wanted to contribute to prevention. I reasoned that perpetrators are the problem. They commit sexual abuse and violence. They were children once. I wanted to learn how children become perpetrators of child sexual abuse. I also reasoned that prevention is fostered when we understand these behaviors from the points of view of perpetrators.

Furthermore, I believed that I can learn some important things if I identity differences between those who perpetrate sexual harm and those who don't. That is what my research has involved—identifying differences between those who abuse and those who do not.

I begin with the words of men who perpetrate to illustrate the challenges of prevention. Their words give an idea of what we are dealing with.

Dan said:

> The only place I found relief was in the act. The rest of the time I felt unworthy, unlovable, heinous. I mean, you know, when I could get a young male to be sexual with

me, and not even, we didn't even have to get to that point, but when I was being shown affection from a young male, wrestling, hugs, doing things together, intimate, intimately. Then I felt loveable. I felt worthy. I felt all of these things that I didn't feel the rest of my life. The ultimate act of that is sex. There was sex. It was always leading to sex.

Jim said:

As long as none of what I was up to with kids was clearly apparent, I could keep getting away with calling it being affectionate and nurturing to kids, and classifying my arousal as, oh, that's just a side effect. This is going on in my head. In my heart I'm not, as long as I'm careful not to show it in my eyes, my face, my voice, my mannerisms or actions, as long as I don't get a hint or a sign of what's going on in me, I can be nurturing and affectionate to kids. That's where I'm getting off on, the experience of being affectionate, etcetera, etcetera, and nobody notices it. That will mean no harm, no foul. That's what I told myself. If I'm not blatant, I don't stick my hands in kids' clothes, between their legs, and what I, abuse, I can't be doing abuse. That's not what I'm doing because that would mean

When we hear people speaking these words and know they mean them, we know we have a problem. What do we do to protect children from them? What do we do to prevent children and young people from developing into persons who experience children in this way? Dan began his sexually abusive and exploitive careers at around age six. Jim began as a teenager. Neither was sexually abused. Both had "good enough" parents.

Furthermore, we know we have a problem when Robert Finn, Bishop of the Kansas City-St Joseph diocese, held for five months the photos that a technician found on a priest's computer. The technician had given the photos to the bishop immediately. The photos were of girls' genitals. The girls were between the ages of 12 and 15. This was during the first five months of 2011, not 25 years ago. I assume that the bishop is a man of good will. What was he thinking?

I have sought to understand child sexual abuse and other forms of violence from the points of view of perpetrators in the hope that what I learn will contribute to primary prevention. I also hope that my research educates people like Bishop Finn to know what to do when they are in a position to prevent offenders from having contact with children while in the employ of a religious institution or any other institution. I hope that my research will have an impact on policy and programs at all three levels of prevention: primary, secondary, and tertiary.

Today, I invite you to think about what child sexual abuse means to you personally. Is child sexual abuse fair to children? Do we have common understandings about what child sexual abuse is? What purposes might common understandings serve? Do we have common understanding about what we could do to prevent child sexual abuse?

One common understanding is that child sexual abuse is wrong. Even some sexual abusers know that.

Dan:

> I hated everything about myself. I thought I was a monster. I knew, I didn't think, I knew I was a monster. I knew that I was engaging in behaviors that I wanted to stop and couldn't stop. That there was just no way because I kept saying, "I won't do this again," and I kept doing it again. It was a constant, (3 sec) constant thoughts, constant, in my head, constant, first thing I think of when I wake up, last thing I think about before I go to sleep. It consumed me.

Some sexual abusers do not believe that sexual abuse is wrong.

Mike:

> At the beginning I guess I used to think that it was good to do this. She was younger. She believed me then. When she started to resist, it turned into threats and manipulation with money. Or "You're grounded," or "You're not going to get anything." "You can't go there.

You can't go here, if you don't do this for me." That nobody would want her, stuff like that. I used a lot of shaming. So it went from caring, what I felt was caring, down to more stronger forcing, towards the last three or four years, actually. June was convenient. She was always there.

There's no stopping once, I started. There was no turning back after that. I just figured that I enjoyed it and why stop. Why tell anybody because I'd get thrown in prison then.

The actual sex—I liked that. Then the control, being in control of her life completely was a thrill for me. I thought about it more than I thought about my wife. She occupied a lot of my time. I don't think of people's feelings. I still have a hard time with that. I'm pretty insensitive about other people. I'm really self-centered. It's just selfish, sexual gratification and that's all. That's about all there is to it.

Some people believe child sexual abuse is wrong, but blame victims for enticing men who apparently are so weak they can't resist hairless, physically and cognitively immature children. One of the many tragedies of this blame the victim mentality is that survivors of sexual violence and abuse experience deep-seated guilt for the part they believe they played in their violation. While perpetrators alone are responsible for these acts, survivors are socialized to believe they must have done something wrong. Many people agree with them.

Prevention

We can learn a lot about prevention from persons who do not become sexually violent and exploitive. Such persons have ordinary experiences. They have secure attachments with their parents most of the time. Parents are emotionally available in general. They have good social skills. Other people like them. They respect themselves and others. They negotiate for what they want. They do not take what they want. They think about the consequences of their behaviors for themselves and for others. Anticipation of consequences is part of what guides their behaviors.

They experience trauma, but they have the support they need to cope. Through experience, they have learned to trust. They turn to people they trust when they are troubled and traumatized. Some may not share their traumas for various reasons, including not realizing that they have experience trauma. Even then, they have the inner resources not to harm self and others in their attempts to manage the effects of their trauma and to feel better. Their concern for themselves and others stops them from acting on self-destructive or other-destructive thoughts.

They may find that sexual sensations are pleasant and help them feel better when they are low, but they have so many other ways of coping with stress and improving their moods that they rarely use sexual behaviors to do so. As they grow older, they experience stronger desires for tenderness, sexual activities, and sexual love. They respect potential sexual partners and negotiate for what they want. Sexual activities typically take place within contexts of trust and secure attachments, often relationships based on love.

People who do not grow to be sexual abusers are exposed like anyone else to ideologies that support violence, entitlement, and selfishness. They have has much encouragement as anyone else to be self-centered and short-sighted. They may have been abused and neglected themselves. They see that some people are rewarded for selfishness and hurting others. They understand that there are beliefs that give permission to take what you want, get revenge, and to react with force when disrespected. These beliefs are not the foundations of their lives. Their foundations are to promote their own well-being and the well-being of others.

My Biography in Relation to my Research

I have spent many years talking to perpetrators of child sexual abuse. I have had to examine my own pro-violence beliefs. For example, I had no idea how firmly embedded the notion of revenge is in me. Only by long-term examination of my beliefs and by latching on to the idea of "Living well is the best revenge"—and implementing it--have a let go of my notions about revenge. I never physically harmed anyone nor was I particularly aggressive verbally, but I did have vengeful thoughts.

Furthermore, I have had to re-live and learn to cope with my own unaddressed traumas, most of which I did not realize that I had until the research led to their surfacing. I have had to examine my own sexual behaviors and see where my sense of entitlement and desire to control others may have been in play. I would not have seen these things in myself had I not seen them repeatedly in the stories that persons who perpetrated told me.

This has been excruciating. I don't know how many people are willing to do this kind of self-examination. From personal experience, I know how difficult it is to change beliefs and behaviors. The intensity of such self-examinations and personal transformation varies according to situations, and it is not easy. I also know how long it takes

Tertiary Prevention

This is what is required for perpetrators if they have any hope of change. Do we have programs that know how to support them in these changes? That create the safety they need to do this deep and honest self-examination and then talk about these terrible, painful issues? The common factors model tells us there are four components of effective treatments. One is treatment techniques themselves. Another is external environmental events. A third is composed of relationships between service users and service providers. Finally, motivation to deal with issues is the fourth necessary component of treatment effectiveness. Treatment is effective when all these factors are in play.

The skills that practitioners involve each of these factors. Practitioners have to know how to form relationships of trust with persons who may not have capacities for forming such relationships. To do this, I believe professionals have to do the kinds of personal self-examination that I put myself through as a researcher. The more self-understanding I have, the more I can understand others. For persons who perpetrate to have the desire to change and courage to examine themselves, they must feel that other people walk beside them.

Professionals who are willing to deal with their own issues have the most promise to be persons who can walk with perpetrators. This does not mean that they say what persons who perpetrate have done is okay. Professionals can be clear to themselves and to the persons they work with that sexually harmful behaviors are wrong because they hurt others no matter how good they feel to perpetrators and how meaningful they may be to perpetrators. Persons who perpetrate usually know this anyway, at least when they are not in the throes of wanting something sexual from someone else.

This also does not mean that we understand sexual abuse and violence as they do, but we do know how it feels to want to do something so badly that we go against our own self-interests and the welfare of others. This does not mean that we have done this kind of thing, but we know how it feels. It also means that we understand sexual feelings and how complicated they are and how mixed in they can be with other desires, such as desire for comfort, affirmation, bliss, and control. Put these understandings of sexuality together with wanting something so much we actually do it despite longer-range consequences and there you have insights into persons who perpetrate.

There you have the foundation for building relationships with persons who perpetrate sexual violence and abuse.

Besides having professionals who are willing to go the whole nine yards with service users, effective treatment programs offer in-depth psychotherapy of various sorts that create the sense of safety necessary for self-examination and change. Change requires the examination of beliefs that are difficult to change because they are tied in with identity, grappling identity issues that may be linked to traumas that persons believe have tainted their identities and thus their self-worth, and contending with the naked fear of being exposed as being deeply flawed. In order to change, persons who perpetrate have to grapple with the deep and painful issues connected to their harmful behaviors.

This requires trust and other capacities related to secure attachments. Since few persons who perpetrate sexual abuse and sexual violence has consistent capacities for the empathy and reciprocity characteristic of secure attachments, it is possible that even with the most qualified of professionals, deep change is long-term and requires much effort.

Besides a trusting and safe treatment environment, effective programs provide many different kinds of psychoeducation over the long-term. Ideas, coupled with intensive self-examination, are important to personal transformation.

Treatment is tertiary prevention. Such treatment has to be individualized. Effective treatment programs do not take a one-size-fits all approach. They apply general principles such as those I have discussed in ways that fit the particular situations of service users.

Secondary and Primary Prevention

Secondary and primary prevention focus on various types of education and consciousness-raising, although psychotherapy could be classified as secondary prevention if persons have risks associated with poor outcomes, among which would be perpetration of child sexual abuse and other forms of sexual violence. We all have these risks; those who do not harm others have protective factors, such as consistent concern for the well-being of others and for themselves, that stops them from harming self or others.

Three inter-related principles can provide a road map for prevention programs. As background to these principles, I share observations I have made during the years of research interviews. I have never interviewed any perpetrator of child sexual abuse or perpetrators of any other forms of violence who had **secure relationships** with care providers, and, as they grow older with a growing social network. That is, they have not consistently shown the sensitive responsiveness, the emotionally availability, the give and take, the anticipation of short and long-term consequences for self and others, and the respect of power and status differentials that are characteristic of secure relationships.

They may sometimes show these capacities, but these capacities disappear as they think about and then action out sexual abuse and sexual violence. They often do not view these acts as harmful at the time they commit them. Rather, they define them as acts of love, even mutual love, and as ways of attaining bliss, fixing how they feel, and any number of non-harmful activities. Some take pleasure in knowing they are cause harm and hurt.

I never interviewed any perpetrators of child sexual abuse and other forms of violence who have **prosocial beliefs that countered antisocial beliefs.** Their antisocial beliefs dominated prosocial beliefs, at least during the times in which they were sexually violent and exploitive. The dominant beliefs during those times are selfish and laced with entitlements. What mattered was what they wanted. If they thought about what survivors wanted, they usually said they believed the survivors wanted what they wanted. Some did not care.

I have never interviewed any perpetrators of child sexual abuse and any other forms of violence whose **sexual behaviors were negotiated, based on mutual respect, and meaningful.** Even one-night stands between generational equals can be respectful with informed consent.

Conclusion

There are three interacting principles that contribute to the primary prevention of child sexual abuse and other forms of sexual violence. They are

- **Capacities for Secure Attachments** develop naturally with the safety of secure relationships in infancy and childhood and continue over the live span.
- **Capacities for Negotiation:** Develops naturally within the give and take of secure relationships
- **Affirmation of the Sweetness of Sexual Behaviors:** Experiences of sexuality as sweet and negotiated require experiences of secure attachments, adults comfortable with their own sexuality, and adults comfortable with socializing children about appropriate and inappropriate sexual behaviors.

I hope we can develop a common understanding of prevention principles. Until we do, it will be difficult to create primary prevention programs. As Prentky, Knight, & Lee (1997) wrote 14 years ago

> If those professionals who deal with the victims and perpetrators of child molestation are willing to harness their collective energy, pull in a common direction, and speak with a single firm voice, properly informed laws can be enacted that will better control child molesters and make communities safer for children (p, 16).

We also must be aware of the importance of secondary and tertiary prevention. The example of Bishop Finn's inaction brought this sharply to my mind. We have to figure out ways to educate Bishop Finn and others in similar positions about child sexual abuse and other forms of violence. People who sexually abuse children must be kept away from children permanently, expect possibly under strict guidelines after years of successful treatment and education that includes the entire system in which those who have perpetrated live their lives.

As long as persons of good will, as Bishop Finn has to be, do not understand sexual abusers of children, those in authority will let other considerations stand in the way of keeping known perpetrators away from children.

Professionals involved in direct contact with persons who perpetrate must have skills needed to promote secure attachments and healthy sexuality. Professionals, therefore, must have capacities for secure attachments themselves and must be healthy sexually. They must do continual reflection and self-examination that builds their capacities to understand persons who perpetrate at deep levels.

By connecting with persons who perpetrate in these ways, they become guides and coaches who provide the sense of safety necessary for the formation of trust. With safety and trust, persons who perpetrate may be able to deal with their identity issues, their fears, their shame, and their beliefs so that they develop capacities for secure relationships, capacities for negotiation, and appreciation of sex as something sweet that can occur between generational equals who give informed consent and have capacities for accepting consequences.

Professionals also must know how to deal with trauma because trauma interferes with secure attachments and not because there is a direct link between trauma and perpetrating sexual abuse and violence, because there is not. Professionals have to deal with trauma so that persons who perpetrate can feel safe enough to deal with beliefs of entitlement. Throughout, professionals must be clear that sexual abuse and violence are wrong because they harm others.

Summary

In summary, child sexual abuse and sexual violence are complex, terrible issues. Their prevention require cooperative efforts of many people from many walks of life. Many of us realize that we need a common language and common direction to do. I wonder what each of you thinks about what you can do. I wonder if you all find the three interacting principles helpful to you. They are general, but, because they are, there are many ways that each of us can put them to practice in particular situations with particular persons.

These principles are like road maps. They provide general direction. They do not show the trees, houses, and lakes. These are the details that general guidelines do not provide. Various kinds of interventions can lead to common destinations. I hope that we share the dream of a common language and goals and that we appreciate the plurality of actions that we can take to work toward these goals.

Note: This is a text of an address I gave at the Minnesota Symposium on the Primary Prevention of Sexual Abuse and Violence: Applying Research to Practice, sponsored by the Minnesota Department of Health, St. Paul, Minnesota, USA, August 26, 2011.

References

Gilgun, Jane F. (1995). We shared something special: The moral discourse of incest perpetrators. *Journal of Marriage and the Family, 57,* 265-281.

Sharma, Alankaar & Jane F. Gilgun (2008). The method to the madness: Myths and realities about perpetrators of child sexual abuse. *Indian Journal of Social Work, 69(3),* 321-338.

Gilgun, Jane F. (2008). Lived experience, reflexivity, and research on perpetrators of interpersonal violence. *Qualitative Social Work, 7(2),* 181-197.

Gilgun, Jane F. (2010). Child sexual abuse: From harsh realities to hope. Amazon, Kindle, iBooks, & Nook.

Gilgun, Jane F. (2010). Reflections on more than 20 years of research on violence. *Reflections: Narratives of Professional Helping, 16(4),* 50-59. http://www.scribd.com/doc/39119048/Violence-Actual-and-Imagined-Reflections-on-More-Than-20-Years-of-Research.

Gilgun, Jane F. (2010). What child sexual abuse means to child survivors. http://www.amazon.com/Child-Sexual-Abuse-Survivors-ebook/dp/B0026ICOUI/ref=sr_1_3?s=digital-text&ie=UTF8&qid=1348867194&sr=1-3&keywords=Jane+Gilgun+what+child+sexual

Gilgun, Jane F. (2010). What child sexual abuse means to abusers. Chapter in present book. http://www.amazon.com/Child-Sexual-Abuse-Abusers-ebook/dp/B001W0Y5AI/ref=sr_1_1?s=digital-text&ie=UTF8&qid=1348867239&sr=1-1&keywords=Jane+Gilgun+what+child+sexual

Gilgun, Jane F. (2010). What child sexual abuse means to women and girl perpetrators. http://www.amazon.com/Child-Sexual-Abuse-Perpetrators-ebook/dp/B003BEDXHO/ref=sr_1_2?s=digital-text&ie=UTF8&qid=1348867315&sr=1-2&keywords=Jane+Gilgun+what+child+sexual

Gilgun, Jane F. (2011). Remove offending priests immediately: What was the bishop thinking? http://www.amazon.com/Remove-Offending-Priests-Immediately-ebook/dp/B005ISPOMS/ref=sr_1_1?s=digital-text&ie=UTF8&qid=1348867387&sr=1-1&keywords=Jane+Gilgun+remove+offending+priests

Gilgun, Jane F. (2011). Values, ethics, and child sexual abuse. http://www.scribd.com/doc/51984539/Values-Ethics-and-Child-Sexual-Abuse

Robert A. Prentky, Raymond E. Knight, & Austin F. S. Lee (1997). *Child sexual molestation: Research issues.* Washington, D.C.: National Institute of Justice. https://www.ncjrs.gov/pdffiles/163390.pdf

26

Lust, Agape, Philia, and Erotic Love: Meanings in Personal Relationships

This article ends the book. I place it here because human beings have a desire for safety, intimacy, and fulfillment. It's part of our DNA. In my long interviews over many years with perpetrators and survivors of interpersonal violence, I have seen this desire consistently. When people feel unsafe, isolated, and unfulfilled, they respond in a variety of ways. Some deal constructively with these unhappy states of being. Others are self-destructive and inappropriate. Still others do things that hurt others. Many of us have a mixture of all four, although one style usually dominates. This article offers of vision of love, intimacy, safety, and fulfillment that does not harm self or others.

Lust is an overwhelming desire to be sexual with another person without forethought, including little or no thought about consequences for self or other. It's delightful to anticipate and blissful to experience, but mindless. Lust can lead to friendship and to agape, but it often leads to unhappy consequences for one or both involved.

Agape is love that involves the active promotion of the well being of the other. Agape is mindful. Agape also can be passionate in some ways, as when parents love children, but desire for sexual union is not part of agape. Agape is deeply satisfying and is a large component of what makes living meaningful.

Some people have a general attitude of agape toward others with whom they are in contact. It is a regard they give freely, without expectation of mutuality. While agape is probably fulfilling, I imagine that such individuals would also have other relationships that are mutual, relationships that refresh and replenish directly.

Philia is friendship that is mutual, but also that is dependent upon circumstances. Persons who experience friendship often have shared interests. Typical friendships are between persons of equal power, but older people can be friends with younger people, if there is mutual respect for the differences associated with age, such as the power older people often have over younger people.

In many circumstances, it may not be possible for friendships to exist when one person has power over another, such as a professor being friends with students or bosses being friends with persons they supervise and have the power to hire and fire.

Friendship can combine with agape so that persons are friends with shared interests and who mutually promote the interests of others.

Erotic love is mindful and involves the active promotion of the well-being of others and that involve the mutuality of friendships, in combination with a powerful desire to be sexual with a person who is of equal status and power. Erotic love is spiritual as well as deeply physical. It is difficult to tell where physicality ends and spirituality begins. The boundaries between physicality and spirituality are blurred. Some people say they are never more themselves and never more fulfilled than when they experience erotic love. Erotic love occurs between equals and is a form of romantic love.

Those who live in love live mostly in agape and in philia. How fortunate they are. Those who also experience erotic love experience it at various points in their lives, but not all day long every day, the way many people experience agape and philia.

At my age, I think about my younger selves and the good fortune I have had in terms of experiences of agape, philia, and erotic love. My experiences of lust were a series of bumbles and stumbles that taught me much. I may not have learned what I learned any other way. At the same time, a few words from my elders might have spared me unhappiness. I hope these words of mine help others to learn something about agape, philia, erotic love, and lust.

Agape and Erotic Love

I can't imagine a human being who does not want agape and philia, that delightful, light, and easy reciprocal connection of one person to another. Most of us experience this, possibly most or all of the time. Philia usually builds over time. There may be an attraction to someone, in the sense that one person feels comfortable with and interested in another person. This can lead to friendships and many kinds of meaningful activities. Friends talk about all kinds of things. They share activities. Friendship can become sacred spaces.

Any chance that another person will become best friends forever, however, requires agape as well as mutuality. Agape is the commitment to the well-being of another, and in friendship this is a mutual commitment.

Once in a while, friends who experience their being together as sacred spaces move toward erotic love. Certain conditions appear to be present when erotic love leads to good outcomes. These conditions include

- both persons are available, equal in status and power, and not committed to another person or to a path in life that excludes erotic relationships;

- both persons are gardeners for the other, cultivating each other over time, watering, sheltering from hail and frosts; their erotic love blooms as a flower does, gradually opening wider and wider in vibrant expectancy; and

- both persons are accountable for any hurtful actions they commit, take responsibility for their actions, recognize the harm they have caused, apologize, make amends, and do whatever it takes not to repeat the harmful actions.

Young people need to know that the path to erotic love is through agape, the active cultivation of friendships that involve of mutual care, fairness, and honesty. Fairness and honesty are important because disagreements and misattunements occur in agape-friendship combinations. That is why accountability and working at not repeating hurtful behaviors are central to relationships that are erotic in the way I mean them.

I recommend at least three instances of breakdowns and repair in relationship in order to trust that the mutuality, honesty, and fairness are lasting. In relationships on their way to erotic love, I recommend the same before giving in to the powerful sexual desire for the other. In other words, don't hop in the sack until you have experienced multiple instances of the above characteristics.

Building relationships of trust takes time. If you do hop in the sack without really knowing and trusting another, be prepared for a range of consequences. This is lust responding to lust, which is sometimes satisfying in the short and long run. It's a crap shoot, however. The odds favor hurt, regret, and guilt.

Mismatches

Sometimes there is a mismatch between agape, friendship, and lust. One person in a relationship may experience agape and friendship for another, while the other experiences lust. When this happens between adults of equal status, such situations may be handled well. The person being pursued says no, and the pursuer respects that boundary. In other situations, rather than accepting no for a response, some individuals insist on their own way and harass others sexually to get what they want. What they want is a satisfaction of their lust.

What pursuers want does not involve erotic love because they are uninterested in mutuality and in the promotion of the well-being of the other. Some may fool themselves into thinking the sex they want with the other is good for the other, but self-deception does not make such thinking true.

There are many situations where older persons, males and females, pretend to have agape and friendship when they only want to be sexual and don't think about what may happen to the other as a result of the sexual activity. I have seen this a lot in my research and in my professional practice as a social worker. For example, older teenage boys or young men do all they can to engage a younger girl in sexual relationships.

They dazzle her with their wit and charm, sweet talk, and promises. The girls and inexperienced young women think these boys and men really care or even love them. They think they are in love. They don't know that agape and friendship compose the road to erotic love, or the romantic love they crave. What they get is a brief involvement with someone who uses them and goes away. This is a mismatch between what the pursuer wants and what the target of his pursuit wants and gets.

This same kind of thing can happen when older boys and men have lust for younger boys and when older girls and women have lust for younger girls or boys. The pursuers want the gratification, satisfaction, bliss, and thrill of sexual contact with someone they lust after. Pursuers are either short-sighted or callous about consequences. Their targets may be too young, too afraid, or too flattered to understand what pursuers are asking of them. They may not see pursuers as the betrayers that they are.

No one has taught the targets of lust to know the differences between lust, agape, friendship, and erotic love. They had no idea the other wants to use them. The other person may see them as conquests whose acquiescence leads to bragging rights. These users puff themselves up at the expense of others and often seek to brag to an audience of like-minded users.

Some of those in lust have other motivations, including believing themselves to be in love. Whether they show agape comes out in how they treat the other after the sexual acts take place. In telling the difference between lust, agape, friendship, and erotic love, actions tell the truth, while feelings and words can lie, even when those in lust do not have these intentions.

Sometimes there is mutual lust, where two people hunger for each other sexually without really knowing each other. Each may have some kind of moral code that guides them to promote the well-being of others, to engage in mutual relationships, and to take good care of themselves. When in lust, however, concern for self and others flies away. What's left is bare naked lust. Sometimes people walk away from such experiences with happy memories, never to see the person again. Sometimes lust leads to love, and sometimes to heartbreak on one side or both.

Sometimes what appears to be lust is not lust, but the workings of a person's broken spirit, where the person mistakes the promise of sexual satisfaction for the satisfaction of friendship, mutual regard, and agape built upon romantic love. Some people are serial bed hoppers, seeking but not finding their one true love. Their task is to figure out how to heal their broken spirits, rebuild capacities for agape and for mutuality, and to avoid acting on their lust.

The harm that persons with broken spirits cause when they act on their lust is similar for those who act on lust out of the desire for a more simple kind of gratification. In other words, broken spirits or not, keep you hands to yourself and your knickers on and covered with outer garments.

Power

From the cradle to the grave those who have power over others require continual education about the limits of their power, the need to respect their power, and the importance of the promotion of the well-being of others, no matter how much they might want sexual satisfaction with others over whom they have authority. No matter what they think they are doing, they must not act on their desire for sexual and emotional gratification. They must think before they act. Evil feels good.

Lust that arises in relationships where one person has more power and authority than the other is always problematic. This can happen in relationships between supervisors and supervisees, teachers and students, parents and children, children and other children, and clergy with adult and child members of a faith community. Any individual with power over others and has any desire, no matter how small, to be sexual with subordinates must seek immediate counsel and ensure that they never are alone with the object of their lust.

Thousands of books and articles are available on these topics. Each instance of lust that is acted upon in power relationships is damaging to the targets. Children typically love their parents. Members of faith communities may respect and feel agape and friendship for clergy, and the same may be so for students in regard to their teachers and supervisees for their supervisors.

Sometimes persons in authority don't realize that they are abusing their authority. They may experience what they think is erotic love and swear ever-lasting devotion. They may tell their subordinates that this is love, as one man did as he sexually used his two year-old daughter or as priests and other clergy do when they abuse children or adult parishioners who go to them for pastoral counseling. Such individuals have huge gaps in their moral reasoning. They do not know the differences between, lust, agape, friendship, and erotic love.

Persons, including children, may be flattered beyond words at the attention of those whom they respect and for whom they have regard. They may experience sexual arousal themselves. Knowing the difference between lust, agape, philia, and erotic love may help many people in such situations to escape the worst of the potential damage the behaviors caused by the lustful desires of those who have authority over them.

I have one more small but final point about the terms, *lust, agape, philia,* and *erotic love. Lust* is an old-fashioned term. No one ever told me what it means and how it feels. I had no idea how good it feels and how powerful the pull to act on it. I couldn't think of another word that fits the idea that a person can want to be sexual with another without regard for the well-being of the targets or the longer term well-being of themselves.

Agape is a Greek word that means charity or care for others. It's rarely used, but I could think of no other word that means what agape means. The term *philia* means friendship as a form of love. The city of Philadelphia, means the city of brotherly love The term *erotic love* is probably old-fashioned and rarely used, but my sense of the term is that erotic love is transcendent love that is also sexual, possibly rare but based upon mutual regard and the mutual promotion of the well-being of the other.

Discussion

Erotic or romantic love builds upon agape and friendship between equals. Agape is the active promotion of the welfare of others of any age without thought of personal gain. Philia at its best is probably a form of agape, but it is a mutual kind of active promotion of the well-being of others. In combination, philia and agape represent a pathway toward erotic love when both persons have equal status and power. Persons who are equal in status and power and who act on mutual lust engage in a crap shoot. Sometimes mutual lust leads to friendship and then to erotic love, but most of the time it leads to unhappy consequences for one or both. Adults who take chances on lust also accept the consequences of acting on their sexual pull toward another.

Mismatches, when one person feels lust and the other agape, sometimes can be handled with simple boundary setting. Situations get more complicated when the pursuer in lust pretends to experience agape and the target trusts the pursuer. Rarely are the consequences anything but hurtful for the pursued and often for the pursuer as well.

Acting on lust when one person has authority over another is always wrong and always has hurtful consequences for the pursued and sometimes for the pursuer. Persons who act on their lust toward those with less power and who may even be dependent upon them have gaps in their moral reasoning. Their behaviors always damage the targets of their lust.

From cradle to grave, persons must be socialized to understand and respect the similarities and differences between lust, agape, philia, and erotic love. They must be socialized to run as fast as they can for counsel when the delights of lust tickle their fancies, especially if the object of their lust has less power than they and may also be dependent upon them.

Note: Thanks to Rev. Dr. Heidi Heidi Joos for speaking about philia.

References

Buber, Martin (1937/2004). *I and thou*. London: Continuum.

Fromm, Erich (1956/2008). *The art of loving*. New York: Continuum.

Gilgun, Jane F. (2011). *Child sexual abuse: From harsh realities to hope*. Amazon, Kindle, & Nook.

Gilgun, Jane F. (2010). Evil feels good: Think before you action. Chapter in present book. http://www.amazon.com/s/ref=nb_sb_noss?url=search-alias%3Daps&field-keywords=Jane+Gilgun+evil+feels+good: Think before you act.

Gilgun, Jane F. (2010). Nujood Ali, 10, divorces 30 year-old husband.

http://www.amazon.com/s/ref=nb_sb_noss?url=search-alias%3Daps&field-keywords=Jane+Gilgun+Nujood

Gilgun, Jane F. (2011). Original sin is not original, but goodness is. http://www.scribd.com/doc/49564877/Original-Sin-is-Not-Original-Goodness-is

Gilgun, Jane F. (2010). Parishioners express outrage at survivors of priest abuse. http://www.scribd.com/doc/30474916/Parishioners-Express-Outrage-at-SURVIVORS-of-Priest-Abuse

Gilgun, Jane F. (2010). Survivors of priest abuse told for 50 years; No one listened. http://www.amazon.com/s/ref=nb_sb_noss?url=search-alias%3Daps&field-keywords=Jane+Gilgun+survivors+of+priest+abuse

Acknowledgements

Many people who have contributed to this book of essays. First of all, I thank the persons who shared their experiences with me. Their words inspired me to persist in my desire to understand violent behaviors and to do something about them.

Many professional gave encouragement, time to talk about the stories, and access to persons whose stories are the foundation of the essays in this book. These professionals are Robin Goldman, Jim Kaul, Steve Sawyer, Steve Huot, Gerry Kaplan, Tom Fuller, Kay Rice, Danette Jones, Nancy O'Hara, Danie Watson, Yvonne Cournoyer, Peter Dimock, Nancy Steele, Pete Rieke, Jim Berg, Cynthia Woodward, Bev Welo, Carol Arthur, Dave Mathews, Dave Wilmes, Donnie Preston, Carlton Linton, Mary McRoy, Becky Mouatka, Hope Melton, Jack Jones, Leslie Norsted, Jodie McElroy, Troy Withers, Antuana Belton, Ed Frickson, Dylan DePrimo, Carolyn Larson, Shanaya Walker, Gala Ingram, Roy Adams, Betsy Brewer, Johnny Allen, and Julie Anderson.

Transcriptionist Nancy Zedlik-Zimney was invaluable, not only in the accuracy of her work but also with the insights she shared over the years. At the University of Minnesota, Dean Keith McFarland, Dean Mary Heltsley, Dean Jean Quam, and Professors Dave Hollister and Jim Reinardy get special thanks for their support, both moral and financial, for this project. Professor Laura Abrams at University of California at Los Angeles listened as I talked through some of the shocking stories I heard. Thanks to research assistants Teresa Connor. Liz Reiser, Laura McLeod, Alankaar Sharma, and Wendy Anderson for their work over the years. Sue Keskinen made many contributions to the research I have done.

The research was funded by the Minnesota Agricultural Experiment Station, the Saint Paul Foundation, the Silberman Foundation, the Allina Foundation, the Ms. Foundation, the University of Minnesota Graduate School, The Center for Advanced Studies in Child Welfare at the University of Minnesota, and the U.S. Centers for Disease Control. Any mistakes and misinformation in this book are my responsibility alone.

About the Author

Jane F. Gilgun, PhD, LICSW, is a professor, School of Social Work, University of Minnesota, Twin Cities, USA. She does research on the meanings of violence to perpetrators, the development of violent behaviors, and how persons overcome adversities. She has published widely in these areas.

She worked at a public Rhode Island child welfare social service agency for several years and then became a professor. She also writes children's books, non-fiction, and articles that are available on Amazon Kindle, Smashwords, and scribd.com for a variety of mobile devices. She has many videos on YouTube that include the landscapes in Northwest Ireland, trail riding in Minnesota and elsewhere, horse racing, pig racing, and more.

Her interests include her horses, Padron's Elegante (Ellie) and Finn MacCool, who are mother and son, her dog Jazz, gardening, photography, cooking, the arts, and spending time in County Leitrim and County Sligo, Ireland.

Jane has a bachelor's and master's in English and American poetry from the Catholic University of America and the University of Rhode Island, respectively, a master's in social work from the University of Chicago, a licentiate in family studies and sexuality from the Catholic University of Louvain, Belgium, and a Ph.D. in child and family studies from Syracuse University. She is a licensed independent clinical social worker.

5
10 mths Wed 12
18   10 Oclock

Printed in Great Britain
by Amazon